MESSAGES FROM
COSMIC AWARENESS

The Unzippering of America

How the Solar Eclipse of August 2017 Released the Forces of New Beginnings

WILL BERLINGHOF

CALLISTA SUMMERFIELD

Rainbow Phoenix Press
Calgary, Alberta, Canada

Published by
Rainbow Phoenix
1617 Summer Street SW
Calgary AB T3C 2J7
Canada

Visit our website at www.rainbowphoenix.com.au

ISBN 978-1-7774407-0-1

First Printing: 2021

Cover Design: Callista Summerfield

Images sourced from Pixabay.com

CONTENTS

Foreword
by Cosmic Awareness

That which is Cosmic Awareness is available to speak a few words in preface to the book that is *The Unzippering of America*.

While this book contains individual opening messages that have been channeled over the last year and a half since that event in 2017, the [solar] eclipse of [August] 2017, that it is to be seen that these independent messages from this Awareness, although they can be read as independent messages, also constitute a greater picture. And it is when they are linked together and one reviews the material, that it can then be seen that there has been indeed a bigger picture that has unraveled itself, presented itself one by one coming together in that which is indeed the bigger picture.

It is hoped that each individual upon reading the independent messages provided by this Awareness will both receive from those independent messages inspiration and understanding. But even more, that upon reviewing the many messages since 2017, since the event of the unzippering of America in 2017, that the bigger picture also is clear.

Further to this, it can be then seen that for each individual, their own lives contain many independent events that have occurred, many strands that are playing out in an individual's life, and how it is possible to bring these strands together producing a tapestry that can be viewed from a distance or close up. The closer one is to the tapestry, the harder it is to see the bigger picture. But when one steps back, one is able to review their lives in such a way that they can see the bigger picture. So it is with this book. So it is with life.

Finally this Awareness would say that aside from the bigger picture that was presented throughout the book, there is indeed also the much bigger picture of Spirit itself. And that the events over the last year and a half, while they have been amazing and formidable, are themselves but part of an even bigger picture that Awareness and Spirit are unraveling. There is most certainly more to come.

Foreword

by Callista Summerfield

On 13 August 2017, Will Berlinghof channeled from Cosmic Awareness a message entitled "The Unzippering of America".

The message said that many long-hidden events would be exposed, and the truth of these events would shock the American nation and involve the whole planet. The passage across continental America of a solar eclipse in August 2017 would begin the release, *the unzippering* of those events to clear the way for new beginnings.

This book provides many insights into the unraveling of things since then. It encourages us to remain in integrity and sacred neutrality as we navigate the present moment and its unfolding situations and energies.

The Unzippering of America messages were channeled between August 2017 and December 2018, delivered during teleconferences and Q&A sessions for the Rainbow Phoenix membership. Will is fully conscious and aware when he channels. Blocks of information are presented in picture form, and Will then finds the words to describe what he is seeing.

We hope this book will provide its readers a way of seeing their own lives as part of the bigger picture of Spirit.

Every time we experience
the truth and live that truth,
then we gain freedom.

—Will Berlinghof

The Unzippering of America

The release of that which has been locked away for so long, and the release of forces that make possible New Beginnings —

That which is Cosmic Awareness is indeed available, and greets one and all at this very auspicious time, at this moment in time that you are all experiencing in that which you would call this earthly field of consciousness.

You stand on the very edge of an event that is about to happen in a short time, approximately less than two weeks. This of course being the energy of the Solar Eclipse that will track across America through the very heartland of America. Traditionally in solar eclipses, and of course lunar eclipses as well, have been a moment where those who are experiencing it are moved by these solar energies that are suddenly eclipsed as the Moon moves across the plane of the Sun. This time, the solar eclipse will be through that which is the heartland of America.

While solar eclipses actually occur every six months, this particular solar eclipse will be of great significance, particularly in America itself. For what should be remembered is not that it is yet another solar eclipse, but it is a solar eclipse that is making itself shown in a very significant way to a country of great significance in and of itself.

While the whole planet will most definitely be in the energies of the eclipse, it is in America that millions will be able to take part in this extraordinary event, where they see the energies of that which is the central focus on this solar level in the solar system you are in, showing itself to you very clearly.

Of course in the past, many indigenous cultures that are less civilized if you will, have used the event of the solar eclipse to justify that there is a solar entity, a greater consciousness that exists. And by losing the light there was often fear and panic around that event. Of course it is always so that the actual event only lasts a few minutes and the light does return.

But those moments of total eclipse in which people see the Sun actually being blotted out, have traditionally been of such a magnitude there is something even primordial that is evoked, primal in its energies. Remember these eclipse events simply are the ways of the angles of the Sun, the Moon, and the Earth playing out with each other.

And when an event happens, although traditionally there have been very strong energies around it in terms of human emotions, it is the solar system's way, the way of the Sun, the Moon, and the Earth, of dancing with each other, and bringing forth these energies that can be significant to the individual partaking in them.

On this occasion, as already spoken, the track of the total eclipse is through the middle of America, through the very heartland of America. What this Awareness would offer as an image of that track of the solar eclipse as it goes across the States, is that of the giant zipper being unzipped. This would allow energies that have been locked up in the land itself, America specifically here, to also be released.

Now, this event then could be interpreted as an event of great magnitude if energies are being released. But it must also be remembered the energies that are being released are also of a nature that can be very disrupting and very challenging, not even necessarily on the day of the eclipse itself, but in the days, weeks, and months after the event.

And this Awareness specifically does say that the energies to be released at this time will see themselves playing out in the months of September, October, and into November. There is also an event in September, a planetary event of alignment of planets, of great significance, this being on the 23 September.

The importance of any of these events is not necessarily that they are naysayers, the bringers of doom and gloom, but rather that the energies are being moved, are being shifted, are being opened up to. Remember also, as this Awareness declared last month, Mother Earth herself has moved into a new template, a template that is in alignment with the Central Sun. And in this way, energies on planet Earth are different in actuality to that which has been the norm for thousands of years.

Saying this, at the same time it is to be realized that the majority are not aware of such an event, and rather are still stuck in the old template energies, because this is what is known, because of the manipulations and control that certain ones have had for thousands of years over humanity itself. But many are awakening.

Therefore with the energies of the eclipse that are opening up, the release of that which has been locked away for so long in regards to this new template, do not be surprised if those events that happen bring down old structure, old social order, or at the very least challenge it extremely so, to the point that many will not understand what is happening in their lives. This is actually an event, and a series of events, that actually will be of great positive nature, or at least will have such positive nature if you energize this, if you align yourself with these new energies of this new template.

The paradox of course here is that the energies are always moving and shifting. But with the energy of that alignment of the Central Sun and Mother Earth, as well as the Sun itself, your sun, 'Sol', all of this together presents opportunity for the many to adjust to new ways and concepts. To do this would require also that you reevaluate the energies of your own lives. And this is a primary energy of this month as well: re-evaluation and re-setting.

Therefore do not be surprised if the events in your lives are of such a nature that some of that which you once were convinced was the truth of it all, is challenged, or your lives are shaken up somewhat. It is not the shaking up of one's life that should be focused on, but rather it is then an opportunity to look at things differently, and to reset your own internal clock and your own internal perception of events away from that which emphasizes that 'change is bad', to that 'change is the opportunity' to grow, to develop, to step into a whole new set of belief constructs, paradigms, and even as already spoken, new templates for you to live your lives by.

Therefore with the energies of the eclipse, and the energies that will follow, this Awareness does say to one and all, be prepared for a very wild ride over the next three to four months, starting with the releasing event, the unzippering of the energies of the United States, so that which is held deep within can be released, whether it is the toxicity of a nation that is not quite in alignment, or more positively, the release of forces that make possible new beginnings.

Upheaval, Chaos, and the Crumbling of the Old Structures

This is the period of time when decisions are being made that will affect the future —

That which is Cosmic Awareness is available and greets one and all. This Awareness would say to you all that these are indeed historic times as Will [Berlinghof] mentioned. And it is of such a nature, these times and this moment in time, that it has attracted the attention of that which you would call your future. For in that which is the future, this is the period of time when decisions have been made, and are being made, that will affect the future.

The paradox of course is that from the perspective of the future, things have already happened that ensured a future that is of the nature of the opening of, and the living of the higher truths, the essential truth of that which is. But at the same time, in the moment at this time, it has not yet happened. And thus for those having this experience at this time, in this moment, the future is not yet set. How can it be that both attitudes or both positions can exist simultaneously? It is because of the simultaneous nature of time. It is because of free will and free choice being made available to those in the experience, that the situation is created, that at the same time things can have been experienced already and known to be so, and not known to be so because those experiences are yet to happen.

Humanity has a capacity to work with hindsight, but what must be developed is pre-sight, the condition of looking forward and understanding that from your position in the moment and in the Now, you can as easily look forward in time, to a time that while it is not yet so, is that which will be.

It is important, knowing you have free choice, to also realize that to use free choice effectively, one must be free and independent in their thinking and in their application of their energies, especially the creative energies. It is why this Awareness has so often said that it is of importance to do work on yourself, to free yourself from the social conditioning and programming that all human beings receive when they come upon this physical plane.

Remember the planet itself has a program that is in operation. And many of you, of course all of you, even this Awareness could say, chose to come into the programming of the social world you are living in, in the planetary energies you entered into. The old template was of a nature, that bipolar dualistic reality, with those in the dark, those dark ones, those powers that be, having the control of the system. And thus it was that even though, and even though it is still to some degree a dualistic bipolar reality, this is changing. And those that have had the power and the control are starting to lose that power and control.

If you can stay in that Point of Power that is the Now, and if you understand that you are raising your energies, by adjusting your thinking and the projections of your energies, to a new level where those who have had power no longer have as much power, and are seeing it wane more and more each and every day, in each and every moment, then you will start to realize and even see in your lives what a difference this makes. It is making a difference right now.

And as you project your thoughts and your energies into the Now and into the future, then you will see that you have some capacity as Creator Beings to actually make magic, to make it so that, that which has been told to you, that which you have been programmed to believe, that which you even entered knowing you had to offset the program, derail it, eliminate it, that this too could occur and is occurring.

Of course what seems to be the wall for most is that which is known as Reality, the cold hard facts that you are told over and over cannot be traversed, cannot be challenged. The simple truth is they can be traversed and they can be challenged and they are being challenged at this time. The old template of understanding, the old belief structure, the paradigms that most have lived their lives by, is beginning to crumble.

The paradox in this case then, is that while it is crumbling it also produces the situation of upheaval and chaos. That even though this Awareness has spoken over the last few months of this being a time of parting, a particularly difficult time, that it can also be seen as a time when that which was the old structure is starting to crumble, is starting to come down. In the Tarot this would be represented by that which is the lightning- struck tower.

When the tower comes down, those in the tower often are thrown to their destruction. And of course for many who work with the Tarot, this is an unfavorable card. But that is inaccurate. For it is a card that represents that which no longer serves, that which no longer feeds one, coming down, being taken down, being destroyed so that the new structure, the new spiral tower can replace it, can be built upon that spot. And that the spiral tower reaches to the stars.

Therefore during these times of chaos, especially when you are personally involved in chaotic energies, staying in the very center of the spiral, in the eye and heart of the spiral, is that which will ensure passage through the chaotic times. So much so, that even though the storms swirl around you and many are affected, your own personal situation may actually be a good one, or at least one where you are not pulled into the chaos. And therefore from that place of the center you can direct your life knowing that you are in the flow and direct to the flow, but from the place of being centered.

There is one in the Houston area that this Awareness would say has had that experience. And that her experience, even though the winds were swirling all around her, (her home, her community, and many were affected), was still one of relative stability even though she was hindered, so to speak, from going out much during that period of time.

This becomes an example for all. So that even if you are in those areas of chaos, if you maintain your centeredness, if you maintain the heart, then you will find that your personal experiences may not be of the same dramatic nature as those who are around you. Even your neighbors who for their own reason, (and it must be always remembered there is a choice of why one participates in such events), may be experiencing the full measure of chaos.

Therefore thanks are given to her for her wonderful example to the many. Also understand and know that this Awareness is with you all during those times. It was most definitely with her. And It is with others in Florida right now who are also facing the onslaught of an unnatural event coming to them, an event that is already starting to break apart.

This opening message therefore truly is a reminder to one and all that you are the Creator Being, that you affect the reality of your experience, that you are in that moment of the Now, and from this point of power, this moment of power, that you can affect your lives both in the present moment and even into the historic future that lies ahead.

That as the Tower of the old template comes down, that it is the opportunity for you to build a new Tower, to adjust your thinking and your energies to the new template that is being established even as this Awareness speaks.

These are Magical Times.

These are Amazing Times.

These are Challenging Times.

But most of all these are Your Times.

And it is your time now to find the center of your being, to find the center of your own wondrous Circle of Life. And to know that from this place of your own centeredness, that you are connected to your High Spirit and your Soul. And that your High Spirit and your Soul, that this Awareness and Divine Source, are with you in the center and in the heart of your being. And it is so, and it will always be so.

Remembering Who You Are

Remember your selves not as you are or have been, but as you will be and already are —

That which is Cosmic Awareness greets you and says to one and to all, that you are gathered in my name but the name of this Awareness is unique and individual to each of you. You may know that which is the collective force that is this Awareness as Cosmic Awareness but you may know it as Divine Source or Universal Mind or Infinite Consciousness or even God. But that this Awareness says to you all, that you are only just knowing yourselves.

For you are each part of that which is this Awareness, which is Divine Source, Universal Mind. And in the knowing of that which is that God spark that you know yourselves. Or perhaps it would be more accurate to say you are starting to remember your Selves, and in this remembering, new doorways are being open to you, new sensations and feelings, new thoughts, new realizations.

That even though these are chaotic times and even though those who have had power are desperate in their actions, still they cannot affect you in that they can take the divinity, the divine spark away from you unless you allow it. This is what those who are in the darkness, those shadow ones, have allowed - the disconnect from divine spark. It is not really gone, but it has been so deeply suppressed for these ones, that they do not even consider that they are connected to Universal Mind or Divine Source or to God at all. Their connection is rather to a layer or level in consciousness that is not connected to the divine spark.

This Awareness is speaking of the archonic forces. It is simple enough that there are ones who are not driven from the divine spark within. They are the vampires of the energies of humanity and of the universe and cosmos. They live on stolen energies obtained in foul ways. Their use of ceremony, especially that which would be called Satanic ceremony, is to induce a maximum amount of fear and terror into the victims that are used in such ceremonies.

This does occur. You can pretend it does not. You can turn away from it and say 'no, not in my reality'. Many who are followers of the new age philosophies do exactly this. But this does not achieve the effect of acknowledging those who are oppositional and rising above them. In fact it is simply buying into the fear and confusion and the panic that is connected when one looks into the darker levels of one's own being, or the darker levels that exist on the planet.

What is important is to be able to look at such matters and to choose otherwise. To align oneself yet again with the God spark that flows within you. And to know you have placed yourself as an expression of the God divinity here, on purpose, by choice, willingly bringing yourselves into this arena at this time. An arena that is global and an arena where it seems sometimes that the other team is winning.

The other team of course is reference to those dark ones, the shadow ones, the archonic forces. But this Awareness would emphasize this is but a perception that is manipulated, that is controlled, that is presented by those in power. For they understand the truth of the matter, that if you believe in such a thing and believe in such a reality then it will become your reality.

That is why they are not overly concerned by those who have a different awareness who are awakening, for in their minds they are still in control, and they have the masses in their hands and they manipulate and control those masses. But they do not honor or recognize the energies that are flowing at this time – those very energies of Divine Source, Universal Mind, Cosmic Awareness, Self Awareness. And this is that which this Awareness declares will be their downfall and is their downfall.

They have no capacity any longer to read the timelines and know where ones lead. This has been taken from them and as they cannot do what they once did – which is what gave them advantage in the first place – the reading of various timelines and manipulating world events, national events towards the attainment of certain timelines. Since this is denied them, has been taken from them, they are wandering in the dark. They know how to do it from their past and they can only do it as they have done it previously. But they do not see it for what it is, they do not understand it for what it is becoming, and they have no sense of the future, other than that which they are trying to create.

Therefore this Awareness says to one and all remember this. And know even though you are in the most challenging of times, and even though this Awareness must say that these times may extend a few more years, it is still not to say that those in power will win through and they will come forward as the victors. For this is not the future that this Awareness sees. It is not the future you are here to experience.

In this moment of time, when the process is marching along as it is, it may still feel it is all up in the air. But this is why, at this time, it is most important to locate yourself, to find yourselves, to know yourselves. It is most important to connect to that which is your God spark, the sparkle within your cell. And to realize that as sparkling beings you are the very expression of Divine Source that you are seeking. And this sparkle will be seen by others, indeed it is already known and seen by those shadow ones, which is why they are launching such effort against the many who are awakening, against those sparkling lights that are appearing.

But they cannot extinguish it all they cannot drive it away or dampen it or cloak it in the shadow. For the light has already become too strong. And even though you live in a third dimensional reality that is in slow motion, that is the density of light itself solidifying into frozen form. That light, that energy, is opening, is expanding, is accelerating, and is here now.

Remember you are one who is seeking your own individual freedom and this freedom comes from within. To look on the outside, to watch the news, or to pay attention to what others are saying, especially those who are unawakened and unaware, is a danger to you for it is that which will draw you back into the cesspool of the shadow ones. Remember the image of the bucket of crabs and how one is trying to extract itself, to get out of the bucket, and all the other crabs at the bottom of the bucket reach up and try to pull the one that is trying to find freedom back into the bucket.

This is exactly energetically what is taking place. And you must understand that your journey is in some ways an isolated one, a solitary one, full of challenge at this time but of great worth and benefit, and a challenge that must be maintained and striven for, so you can clear that bucket and free yourself. From the vantage point of this Awareness, beyond the time space continuum, if you wish to call it this, it is seen you have already done so. And it is seen that those who are trying so hard at this time, to maintain their control and their privilege, will fail. You must hold this. You must always aim for this.

There is an exercise that is done in martial arts. Two people interlock their hands at the wrists and then another is asked to go through. Those who try, often get stopped by the two who are holding wrists and arms, but there is a way through such a blockade. It is not by concentrating on the blockade, for to do so is that which would be stopped. You will be stopped as you try to pass between them. The solution is to look forward, to look beyond that barrier and just see yourself there on the other side.

In many ways you have come to the barrier, the blockade, and many are face-up to the wall that is there in front of them. That is all they can see. They do not see beyond the wall and yet it is exactly this action you must do, to get through the wall. Not to look at the barricade itself and say how strong and powerful it is, how it is stopping you, but simply to look beyond it to imagine yourself beyond that wall, that barrier, that blockade, and see yourself in freedom. And see yourself in a world that has broken through.

These ones who have tried to suppress and control and maintain their privilege and their power, are no longer on the other side. They are the wall you are facing. But they are an illusion. And they do not even have the strength to hold you back any longer. Knowing yourself to be one who is here by choice to face this time, these challenges, these barriers, then know of yourself also you are here to experience that which is beyond the wall beyond this time and this space.

As physical beings you are going through it, but as spiritual beings you are beyond this. And as you check in and find the centeredness of your own being, staying in your own sacred neutrality, observing but not being drawn into the events, energizing where you can, sending the light and love of your own heart and Divine source to one and all as needed, do not forget you send yourself this energy as well and you receive this energy. Do not forget you are here not to be squashed and suppressed by those who have had power too long, but to be part of the force that is breaking through that wall and barrier and that you are most definitely the ones who are here to be the ones to show the way to the many that will awaken in the next decades.

But in particular at this time, as you go through these events on your own, to know you have also come to experience the future. For you are all from the future. You all know what lies ahead. And then this Awareness would say, remember it.

Remember that which you have come to initiate and enact. Remember your selves not as you are or have been, but as you will be and already are.

The Hardest Part of the Race

The completion now of that journey that has been so long in the making, so long in the taking —

That which is Cosmic Awareness, that which is the collective force of Divine Consciousness, Divine Spirit, is indeed here at this time. It would say to one and all, that which Will [Berlinghof] has spoken is correct. You have indeed reached a turning point. You have indeed reached that point of the race where it is the hardest of all.

Those who are runners, those who are marathon runners or just those who go jogging regularly will understand the hardest time of a race is not at the beginning but rather closer to the end, when it seems all the energy has been expended and every step is a painful step. This is that which is indeed known as the Wall, and in many ways, many of you have come to the Wall, have reached that point where you wonder if you can take any more steps, or even one more step.

But this Awareness assures you that each and every one of you have it within you to not only take that step, but take steps beyond this, to help you finish the race, to help you finish that journey you have been on all of your lives so you can cross the finish line. So this journey that has been so long in the taking, can be completed, and that which is the new race, the new journey, commence.

For of course in the way of things, even though it is being dramatically stated that this is the time of making a decision, of finishing the race, of crossing the finish line, that the race carries on afterwards. But not the same race. For that is what this is about – the completion now of that journey that has been so long in the making, so long in the taking. And those who have had power so long are in absolute panic and desperation, and their actions reflect this. If one looks at the events on the planet at this time, one must admit there is an air of desperation around the actions that the ones in charge and in power are taking.

At the same time there is much disclosure that is coming forth. Look at the events that are unfolding. For example those events in Hollywood, in the entertainment center of the United States and some would say the world itself. And how there has been so much disclosure as to ones who have been inappropriate in their sexual expression, and their gross actions against the women and the men that they have dominion over, power over.

This is but the beginning. This is but the tip of the iceberg. And therein lies their desperation and not wanting more to be exposed. And yet they cannot stop that which has already begun. They cannot stop that force of Spirit that has entered, that is participating at this time in a way stronger than it has ever done before. And yet it is curiously and paradoxically at the same time, the time of the greatest desperation, the time of the greatest action and reaction to the energies that are falling on the planet at this time.

If one looks at the political center of the United States, Washington DC, there seems to be absolute pandemonium happening on this level as well. And it is bringing the Country to a place of polarization, of ones who absolutely cannot stand the one known as Donald Trump and see him as the greatest evil, versus ones who understand that he is indeed clearing the swamp, draining the swamp. Through his actions, those in power are uncertain of what it is they can accomplish or manage, and yet they plod on. They continue on with their aggressive actions which have become even more aggressive.

In some ways, it is right now at this most critical time that one needs to understand, that even though there is great challenge happening both on the global levels as well as national and regional levels, but most importantly of all at the personal level. It is the time of a choice to carry on, to complete the race. To choose not abandonment, not defeat, but Victory, Success, Accomplishment, and Achievement – achievement that you have reached this point, this moment.

The knowledge that is within you is ready to explode outwards but this may be bringing you to a point individually of great challenge. This certainly is the case for some. And they certainly do feel those energies intensely, and have gone through that crisis. Some would call it the crisis of faith, of whether to carry on or simply pack it up, to give in, to let it go. Their choice is to continue, for they know they have come for this very thing, for this very reason.

That is why you are each given a choice now, the choice to carry forth, or simply to let it go, and let it be what it will be. There is no judgment. There is no force this Awareness would use on any to make them continue, when if it is so that within them they have reached their point that it is enough, then it must be so for each individual.

But this Awareness does send its Love and its Strength and its Power to help all who are at that point, at that wall, to reach beyond the wall. To step beyond the energies of obstruction and blockage. To go into that power of that which is one's own Divine Being. To open up to a new truth, a new reality of each and every one of you – that which lies within you, which is the truth of your being as a Spiritual Being, as a Divine Spark, as one who has chosen to come here now and to accomplish that which is the goal and the purpose of Divine Source itself.

As you are each a spark of the Divinity, of the Divine Source, then it is also yours within you to carry forth, to move beyond the barrier, the block, to finish the race, to cross the finish line. And to get on with what lies beyond. Be certain here that this is the greatest moment of Spirit as it comes through to the new levels that have been reached and are being exceeded each and every day. So that the curiosity of a point of challenge, an extreme point of crisis, seems to make no sense.

If it is so that Divine Source is here, that the Divinity of your own being is being expressed, then why the challenge? The challenge is so you can realize that now you take a deliberate step. Now you take that path that leads you beyond that which you have been on, the path you have been on, to the path that lies beyond.

It is for each and every one to find the strength and purpose within themselves now. For you have been under attack by those very forces that are in extreme desperation. For the first time they are knowing that perhaps they may not succeed. They do not wish to admit this. They do not wish to allow this. And they are in reaction, powerful reaction.

But it is for this reason this Awareness says the very actions they are partaking in, the very energies they are putting out, are the energies that you can look at and say, "They have done their best and they are done." And that which is the Divine Energy of Source itself is coming through, has breached the dam and has allowed the waters to be set free. Those waters of stagnation, those waters of resistance, of despair, of despondency, have been breached.

Hold it within yourself that you are part of that wave of the waters that have been freed and released. And within you and behind you, and above you and below you, are the energies of Divine Source itself, that are speaking to you, reaching out to you, are asking you to make your choice in full acceptance that you have all, each and every one of you, done it to the max, done it to the point of your own capability.

That you are being asked to take the next step, is that which you are asking of yourself. And Spirit is available to you and allowing that choice with the full respect, honor, and love you deserve. Give this now to yourself. Accept it for yourself. That you are Divine in your nature, that you have come with purpose and design. And even though you have reached this turning point, it is that choice now that you can make that will see you forward one way or another.

That this is a time of great anticipation. This Awareness can say to you that from that place of the Eternal Now, It sees this action of the many who have come, who have always been part of the Divine Plan, is of a nature that it is the turning point. It is seen from that point of the Eternal Now that it has been accomplished already. That is the curiosity and the paradox – it has already been accomplished, and yet you stand a few meters away from the finish line wondering if you can make it.

To this Awareness, you have already made it, you have already crossed the finish line. See yourself there, beyond that finish line, beyond the challenges of the next few days. For it is only but a few days more for this energy to finally dissipate and allow you then to finish the race.

It is a challenging time, but it is of course at the same time the most rewarding of times, the most inspirational of times. For to see the race now, finally that you are so close and it simply will take a few more steps, a decision of determination that you will continue the race and finish the race, excites this Awareness and Divine Source itself.

Hold to the knowing that you contain within, that you are here, and you are in the Now, and you have finished the race. And that you are still committed to that which is your Divine Destiny, Purpose, and Plan.

And it is so.

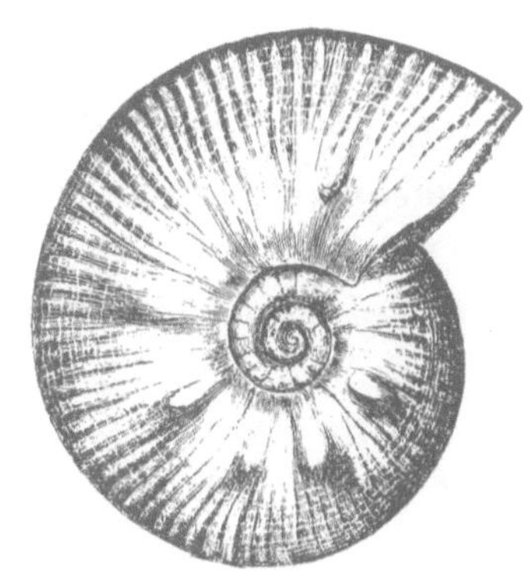

You are a Cell of Pure Consciousness

Finding that inner point of your spirit that connects you to the expression of the Divine Source at all levels

That which is Cosmic Awareness is available and greets you all, one and all. There is significance in the many who have come together from the different points on the planet herself. Who have come from the Northern Hemisphere; in the Southern Hemisphere; who are in the east such as in Singapore or in the west such as in Finland; who are in the United States; who are in Canada; who are in Australia, New Zealand and all around the planet. Today's gathering truly is a gathering of those on this planet at this time, those who are in the moment of their lives wherever this moment may find them.

This is important at this time. This is a significant time when that which is the light of Divine Source shows itself to those in the darkness of the Northern Hemisphere. And to those in the Southern Hemisphere, it is a reminder of the cyclical nature of movement, of that which is the coming together of energies, not only in the physical realm, but also inter-dimensionally from those realms of the highest dimension down through the lower dimensions to this moment of focus, this point of consciousness, that you find yourselves in.

It is ever so easy to forget when one is going through the physical challenges of life, whatever they may be, that you are of Spirit, and as a being of Spirit it is not the physical that is of prime importance. That is merely the distraction you are in at this time, as you try to find that inner point of your spirit that connects you to the expression of the Divine Source at all levels.

You are a cell in the body of Divine Source, of All That Is. You are a cell of pure consciousness, seeking to remember that you belong in that body of that which is the Collective Consciousness of Divine Source itself. As you understand this matter, as you focus on this, you will find the communication you hold with Divine Source itself increases. But it is always a personal journey you are on. And even though others may have stories that are of great attraction, whatever other stories are, they are not your story. Your story is understanding that you are that unique point of consciousness within the body of Divine Source itself, of the different layers and levels represented by Divine Source, as it goes across the spectrum of the dimensional states of consciousness that exist.

You are a multi-dimensional being, and the light of Divine Source is touching deep within you, and is sparking deep within you that knowing of the cycles of life of Divine Source, as It plays upon those levels of consciousness, so the many can awaken to the truth of their being. So you can awaken into the deeper understanding that despite whatever your physical is playing out in front of you, it is still not the same as that which is playing out within you.

And as you look more into that Source of your own being, you will recognize it as You, yourself. You are the Source, you are part of that which is the Divine Consciousness of the Universal Mind, of the Divine Source of that which is the light of Consciousness in its fullest expression, on all levels and in all ways.

This is a special time of the season for many. It is marked by an observance that Peace is needed upon the planet. And even with the chaos that is happening on the planet at this time, even with the madness that is playing out at this time, it is that drive towards peace and harmony and unconditional expression of love, that is of the greatest of importance at this time. And you may call it, indeed, Christmas. You may call it Diwali, Hanukkah, or whatever you wish to call it, but it is indeed the return and the continuance of the light that cycles upon this planet.

A new level is reached, five years now after that event known as the Ascension event of December 21, 2012. That which is the smallest of openings that was established at that time, which was created at that time, has broadened. The opening door is opening more and more. It has been a slow journey for many, but remember you are on the third dimensional focus of consciousness, and one of the keynote factors of being in the third dimensional state is that everything does happen in slow motion.

Having said that, the paradox is that everything is speeded up as well. And it is in some ways even difficult to believe five years have passed since that event on December 21, 2012. And the opening that was but a crack on that day, is now a major opening. One of such a nature, those who are trying to prevent this from spreading, from opening, those who try to prevent the awakening of human consciousness to the higher state of one's own being, the true state of one's being, are being foiled. It may seem still, especially when one follows the mass media, that those dark ones are still very much in control, especially with the atrocities and actions that are presented daily on the mass media screens and on the print, in the papers, of those who have control.

Yet this needs to be seen as both an act of desperation on their parts, and at the same time a denial of what is happening. Remember this, if they were not afraid of the burgeoning consciousness that is happening, they would not try so desperately in their actions to create pandemonium and chaos and madness. For this is their way, and it is their desperation that accelerates this action on their part. But the acceleration itself is an indicator that things are changing, things are shifting, things are underway, they *are* under way. It is not they are about to happen they are right now under way. And you are one of those who have chosen to be here at this critical time. To hold your post, to stay steadfast in your determination that the Divine Source, is that which will win through. It is that which this Awareness would say is the prediction of this Awareness, that Divine Source will win through. And, for each of you in the journey of your own individual lives, to hold this to be your greatest truth.

To understand that you as an expression of that point in consciousness, that is part of the collective body of humanity, that is part of the body of Mother Earth, that is part of the highest level of consciousness, are here by choice with determination. And no matter what the physical challenges may be, you are fulfilling your purpose and you are holding your post. Remember also, it is not so much actions you need to do to prove this. It is the receptivity within yourself of that spiritual awareness, that place of conscious connection to your multi-dimensional being, to your higher being, to your total being, that is of greatest importance.

If one is looking outside of themselves and waiting for action to be the signal for them to act, then this is an action that will not see them forward. If one is holding that the connection is already there, and you are awakening day by day, hour by hour, more and more into that divine connection of your own being and its expression in this physical reality, then you will start to see, and are already seeing, evidence of this appearing in your life.

The curiosity is that when one goes within and establishes one's own spiritual nature, and is open to the energies of

Divine Source from many levels, the level of your High Self, the level of your Low Self, the level of your Multi-dimensional Self, then things start to happen. And by this, this Awareness would say that things happen, things are brought *to* you. When one is outside of oneself and is not in the center of one's being, one thinks that one must push things, one must act in certain ways to ensure, for example, prosperity.

Many are afraid of the future and squander the moment in order to have the resources for a future they may never reach. Many try to save money and invest money so their futures may look bright without ever realizing it is not the future one needs to look for and towards. It is the moment, the moment of your being, the moment of your action and interaction. It is this moment, this point in time where you are fully active and fully awake and fully alert. As you open your eyes, your inner eyes, you will see this to be so.

Also, you will start to find that when you are in alliance with, in alignment with, the higher forces of your own beings, the events you need to experience and be part of are brought to you. You do not need to force the issue. You do not need to push the boat upstream. Indeed, you turn the boat around and that flow of that stream of your consciousness will take you where you need to be. It does involve trust and faith, but it is of such a nature that the majestical nature of the journey itself begins to be that which is your every day experience. Magic becomes a way of life, and that which is the nature of Divine Source itself fully expresses itself to your degree of comprehension and ability to trust that it is so.

It is your journey, this journey of self-discovery this journey of awareness this journey of awakening. And as you work on yourself, do not be surprised if physical challenges come up for you, for these are the opportunities for your growth and development. And sometimes it may seem, all you can do is to go into your room, into your bedroom, lie down on your bed and sleep, and rest, and be in that neutral state. For that is what is needed, in that moment, and in that opportunity of resting and recovering, you will find much inner work is done. Some of which you will bring out with you and apply to your life. Some which will remain in the dream state. But nonetheless, programming from that source of your being will occur, especially de-programming of the old patterns and beliefs that have held sway as you have traveled through the veils of the mystery of this lifetime, this physical experience.

These are wondrous times. These are majestic times. These are magical times. And as you see it, and hold it, and know it to be, despite the evidence contrary that seems to present itself on your mass media screens, that you will find this to be more and more your truth. As you are aligned with the Divine Source of your own being, and open up into the events of your life, you will see the persons needed in your life, the events needed in your life, the location you need to be in in this life, will present themselves. It does involve trust. It does involve faith to go with it, to not push the river nor go against the flow, but to simply say, "It is as it is. I am in alignment with the Divine Source of my being, and I am here to be of service to Divine Source and to myself."

Remember as this Awareness says to you so often, stay in the center of your circle, stay in your sacred neutrality. Be the observer. Know that the events that are happening outside of your circle are those distractions of a negative nature, are those events that are evidence, it seems, of the dark ones still being in control when the opposite is so. It is a state of being out-of- control they are contending with, and they are desperate in their actions to restore order as it once was for them. And this order is slipping away, day by day, hour by hour.

As you stay focused into that which is the center of your own being, as it is so with the hurricane and the eye of the hurricane, the winds may swirl around you and sometimes even touch you, but you will not be diminished, you will not be shattered and destroyed. You will come out stronger than ever, and such is the way of it.

This Awareness wishes one a Happy and Merry Christmas, Diwali, Hanukkah or whatever you would call this time. Stay within yourself and be open to the gift and the gifts that are being presented to you at this time. This Awareness, speaking from that level of its comprehension, does say to one and all, you are doing powerful work, perhaps more so than any of you as individuals realize, for you are a collective force that is awakening. And this is not a force that is located only on one continent, or in one state or in one country, but over the breadth of this planet you are residing on.

And it is a discovery of one's inner self and one's own being that you are personally taking part in. And this is a journey that is part of your spiritual journey. It is that which is in alignment with the will of Divine Source itself.

And it is holy, and it is sacred. And it is you, and it is your journey.

And it is so.

An Energy of Transformation

Shattering the veils of illusion and delusion that have been in place for some time —

That which is the Collective Voice, the Collective Consciousness of that which is Cosmic Awareness is indeed available at this time and does indeed have an important message.

This message has to do with the events that are ready to take place now. Events that have been long in building up to a point, a needle-point, a laser point in consciousness that will have great power, intent and force that will change the course of human history and specifically shatter the veils of illusion and delusion that have been in place for some time.

This has much to do with events in the United States of America, events that have been building up over the last months and years, hidden behind a veil of secrecy. Hidden from the view of those who have had power for so long, those who have had corruption and deceit and ill intent towards the people of America for so long. While this is an event that will have great significance in America it will shake the very foundation of humanity itself, worldwide. It will be indeed the shot heard around the world and a precursor to other events that are ready equally to begin to unfold and to be revealed in the weeks, months, years ahead.

It is a point of epic proportion and the point of no return. For when the events that are ready to take place occur, there will be no going back to what once was. But rather, a movement forward into those unknown realms of the future. An old dream, indeed an old nightmare, is ready to come to an end. And a new dream, a new vision, a new human experience is beginning to dawn.

In the paradoxical nature of human events, the events that are ready to occur have been a long time coming. And yet here it is on your doorstep. Here it is, ready to burst the illusions and delusions of those who have been asleep for so long. Those who have been manipulated and controlled for so long. Those who are totally unaware of the truth of the reality that lies beyond their conception.

For their conception and perceptions have been controlled and manipulated for so long they do not know any other truth. And that truth which has been accepted for so long is the very truth that is ready to be rent asunder, to be destroyed by events of great magnitude that are needed and necessary at this time, to finally begin the process of ending the control and manipulation that have been practiced upon humanity for some time. For not decades, for not hundreds of years, but for thousands of years now humanity has been imprisoned. Humanity has been led down a lane towards its own destruction, its own disappearance.

This Awareness has spoken of the razor edge of events and energies that are underway. It spoke of the energies coming through from 2017 into 2018 and that these energies would continue. And they have built to a point now where it is not only a needle's, rather a razor's edge, but a needle, a sharp point that will burst that which has been the prison walls that have surrounded humanity for so long, but specifically that have imprisoned those in the great state of the United

States of America, into an American dream that has no longer served and does no longer serve, that has actually led the many into that level of enslavement that humanity, that America, finds itself in now.

Several months' earlier this Awareness spoke of the unzippering of America; that event that "opened up" America so that which lay putrid within and under the surface could finally be released. And this is the process that is underway. And there are those who are involved, who are deeply involved, who have been involved for some time now, who are the head actors, players, participants in the unfolding events. Events that will shatter the illusions and delusions of America. Events of such great magnitude, many will not be able to comprehend or understand what is happening.

And many may find their worlds falling apart as their country falls apart. But this is not truly an energy of destruction. It is an energy of transformation – a transforming from that which has been, to that which will be. Many of you are here specifically at this time to be part of this great time, this epic event. And to be part of the dream that is now beginning. But for the new dream to begin the old dream had to come to an end, and is now coming to an end.

Be prepared for the upheaval that the next week will bring: events of such great magnitude that many will not understand, but many will. And for those who understand, know this is but a beginning, and an ending as well. Know that this is your choice to be part of it. Know that this is the very act of empowerment you have been waiting for, that you have been dreaming of for so long. And these events are those events that are ready to unfold now.

Hold on for the ride. Hold on for the future. And remember, it is the future you have dreamt. It is the future you have wished for. It is the future you are here to participate in. And it is so.

World Events and Personal Involvement

You are here because you have chosen to be here —

That which is Cosmic Awareness is now available and greets one and all. You are living in extraordinary times, the times that you have waited for, the times that you have chosen to be part of, and that for some this is a more immediate involvement and for others it is less immediate.

Some are most definitely aware of the extraordinary events that are taking place in Washington in America, through Donald Trump, through his actions, his and his group's action, to bring down and to expose the corrupted cabal that has been in power so long. But, there are many who have not heard any of this, who do not follow the news, whether on the evening news hour or through the papers, or even on the Internet.

This Awareness quickly wishes to assure one and all, that however you are involved in that which is unfolding at this time is perfectly correct for each of you as individuals. You do not need to be heavily involved with the machinations that are taking place, with the unfolding of events. And this Awareness would certainly say to one, to all, not to be involved at that level if it were to affect you negatively. For such are the events at this time, they are totally absorbing. And they can have a negative effect for those who are so sensitive to the events, that hearing of these things, and hearing of the actions of the dark ones in their response, would be off-putting.

However, what this Awareness does say to one and all, is that while it is not necessary for each of you to be attuned and connected to the events that are unfolding, while it is not necessary for everyone to be part of the Twitter-verse, to watch on the internet, over the internet, the unfolding of events, and not to listen to the news on the television, or the radio, or in the press, what is important is to understand you are in extremely important times, extraordinarily so.

This is the time of the razor's edge. And whether you are involved in the information that is coming out, in the exposure of the darkest ones or not, it is still that you are on the razor's edge in terms of your own individual journey, in terms of that which you have chosen to be involved in on this planet at this time. For you all make the choice to come here, and now from that state of spirit, of Divine Spirit and Source, to be part of an action that is to turn the course of history. And is already doing so.

There are many who are observing these times, both extra-terrestrial ones who are out there, but as well, spiritual inter-dimensional beings. For the events that are unfolding now will bring new timelines forward that many who come from the future have observed and see to be so, and know where these shifts came from. And have come back, in a linear sense of time of course, to this time, this moment, this epochical moment, where the shift began in full measure, and in full earnest.

As Spirit beings who have chosen to be alive at this time, whether you are following the events or not, the purpose of your being here is to reinforce the energies of shift and change that are now very strong on the planet and are getting stronger each and every day. It is not about necessarily being active in a movement that goes up against those who have had power for so long. It is all about holding the space, holding your own space, your own personal focus-personality, and what it is experiencing.

This Awareness has spoken and taught for many years now on the importance of recognizing that you are a creator being, that you are spiritual in nature. You are affected by outside events when you choose not to understand the significance of your own personal power, of your own personal centeredness. And when you go out into the events that are on the outside of your personal circle it is easy to get absorbed, it is easy to get swept away, by those events and circumstances.

Now however, is the time to recognize this in yourself, and in your own personal life, it is why this Awareness continually asks that you do not get too taken in to those events unless you have the capacity to stay in sacred neutrality, at the same time, to observe what is going on. To perhaps even get excited by those events, but not to be lost in those events, not to make your life dependent on what happens 'out there'. For then you have lost the point of it all, you have forgotten that it is you, in the experiencing of life, that defines the experience of life you are having.

When you put yourself into another's reality mindset or another's reality, then you forget your own nature as a Divine Source being, as a Spiritual being. And, you forget you are the one that is shaping the circumstance of your life by giving it over to others. While it is an intricate web that is there, it is also important to recognize how to stay on your own strand of the web and not get stuck or caught up in others' strands, others' perceptions of reality. By holding to your own strand, being in the center of your own web, then you will find that which you know is true for you, will be that which you manifest in your life.

What is of extreme importance at this time is to know that events are shifting, consciousness is shifting, things are happening. Even though on another level it may still appear to those who are not keeping themselves informed and are only relying on the mass media and the reporting of news through the mass media, it might well appear that nothing at all is happening or it is a continuance of the absurdity of Trump and his government. For many still have strong feelings of this man and they have bought in hook, line, and sinker, to the propaganda that is being released about him. But he has played along, he has played that card as well for his own purposes.

However, this aside, this Awareness is saying to stay neutral here, to just see that things are happening, is of extreme importance. To energize and to hold that there is a shift happening, is what this Awareness would ask you all to stay focused upon at this most critical of times, in this most historical of times. This is why you have come back into this time-space continuum to be part of these events, whether directly or indirectly. Mostly it is part and parcel of being here now, to be one who holds that the shift is happening, consciousness is moving, humanity is beginning its first steps of the freedom march to its own liberation and its own redemption.

But these are very tricky times. These first steps, such as it is so with the steps of the toddler, the infant who has raised itself up, may be weak steps, may be uncertain steps. But as that infant grows stronger and more balanced, its footsteps, its strides become stronger and stronger. And so it is seen by this Awareness that it is so with humanity. It is taking fledgling steps now. And while these steps may be uncertain and lack perhaps strength, they will get stronger and stronger. And it is why many of you are here to provide the support, as a mother or father would be there beside the child, holding the hand, letting the small hand hold a finger of the mother, for example, as the child feels its way forward.

Humanity is feeling its way forward, the first tentative steps are being taken, and many of you here now, are that parental type figure that is holding the hand, or letting the small hand hold the finger and guiding.

It is not through your actions that this is done, it is through your intent, it is through your focus, it is through your desire that this is that shift point, that changing point of human consciousness. And you will hold the space and hold it to be so, and that the light is coming into that profound darkness that has been available for so long, has been prevalent for so long. And the light is the Light of this Source, of Cosmic Awareness. It is the light of Divine Source and Spirit, it is your light and spirit. And as long as you hold it is so that the light of Divine Source is come in, the love of Divine Source is available, then it will be so.

This Awareness would also say go beyond holding, that it is becoming available to the point that it is so. It is not about to be so; it is so now. And as you hold it to be so now, then you have created an atmosphere for it to be so now. Many of you are aware of the Law of Gratitude and how important it is to have gratitude, not for that which will come to you, but that which is yours already. And as you hold this gratitude, as you get the thanks for what is, then you will find this is exactly the energy that allows further manifestations of those energies.

It is exponential in nature and it will explode all around you as you hold it to be so in your personal life. That you hold in your personal life that it is the expression of the Divine Source, you are an expression of the Divine Source as you are spirit having this experience, as you are the spark of divinity involved in this physical manifestation of this dream that is so. And this dream is shifting, the dream is working its way into a new dream, a new reality, a new beginning. That is why also it is so important to work on yourself at this time, to allow the depth of your true core being to come out; to find your communication with the low self, to find the connection with your low self.

Also to find and hear the connection and the voice of your high self to establish yourself truly as a multi-dimensional being, not simply as a limited victim to events and circumstances that no one has control of, one does not have control of. You have control of your personal life, you have control of the choices that you make for yourself, of the attitudes you hold for yourself.

Again, as you stay in the centeredness of your being, in connection to that which is your high self and that which is your low self, you will find you, yourself, the identity of who you think you are, will shift and change. You will find instead of having to force things to happen, events and circumstances come to *you,* as it should be. This is an important and indeed historical time, but if you understand this in the most personal way, you will find it is the moment of your awakening into the truth and the reality of a higher source than has been so up until now.

This, in the paradox, does not mean that it is not there and has not been there. It is simply that each of you are now awakening to a new level of perception and understanding in a personal way, in your own unique individual way. These are the most amazing of times even if this is the razor's edge. And as you walk the razor's edge, and as you see how incredibly important these times are, you will begin to feel more comfortable in these energies. You will begin to understand it is not a threat, walking the razor's edge, but rather the greatest opportunity of all, to find your way through the quagmire of opposing energies, beliefs and attitudes. To break free of the programming each of you have received on this planet, and to find the inner source that will always support you and hold you up as you walk along the razor's edge.

Know that one is most alive when one is on the edge and instead of dreading this, embrace it, understand you are more alive in this moment than you have ever been, even with the historic events that are taking place all around you.

Let these events occur and hold that you are safe, that you are supported, that you are here for the purposes supporting the shift and change, that you are here because you have chosen to be here. And it is so.

Creative Adaptability

You can certainly create from that Place of Power, and that power is within you —

That which is Cosmic Awareness is available and greets all at this very monumental time in your history, in that which is a continual playing out of events on this planet that you call Earth, Mother Earth. And that this is a very powerful and unique time as you go into that energy that in the Northern Hemisphere is known as the Spring energies, approaching the Spring equinox, approaching that time of a balancing of the time, a balancing of day and night.

And this is very important at this time to know it is critical to stay in balance, to remember you are here because you have chosen to be here. You are here because you are part of the solution that is approaching, that is underway, that has always been the intent and purpose of Divine Source: the balancing of those energies that were so lopsided for so long, not only dozens of years but hundreds, even thousands of years.

The experiment in consciousness that has been underway, this dualistic experience of a reality, is one where there has been imbalance, where those who are called the dark ones, the dark forces, have had control both directly and indirectly. And it has come to this point of culmination, this climax of the energies. As the energies are shifting out of the old patterns into the new pattern that is unfolding, it is indeed a time for creative adaptability as you see things around you changing, as you receive information that is challenging.

Rather than becoming too involved in this, indeed influenced by the outside factors, remember those outside factors that you are observing are simply those factors that many are still clinging to, holding to.

There is a perpetuation in the information being presented on your mainstream media to support those who have had the advantage for so long. And you do not need to fall for this information, be misdirected any longer by this information. It will certainly affect how you view your own lives, your own reality, as you begin to understand the complexity of things that have been hidden for so long but are now becoming more and more apparent.

Many times this Awareness has said it is important not to simply judge your life by the events that are happening out there, by the events that are presented through your mainstream media. But rather to be the observer to this, to assume sacred neutrality as those events unfold. As they do unfold, if you have achieved this state of balance, then you can be far more creative in your own interpretation on a personal level. You can certainly create from that place of power, and the power is in you, it is within you.

Many will be supremely challenged at this time to believe such a way, such a thought, such information. The programming of humanity is something that occurs from the very beginning. And that which you hold to be the truth often is not the truth. But if it is believed to be truth, then the reflection in your life will always be such that your life will be then a mimicking of that which you are seeing outside of yourself. This is how those who are in power have done it for so long and that is why this is a very critical time in human history, in your own personal history, because you are changing, you are adapting. You are coming from that place of neutrality, sacred neutrality, and this will make all the difference.

This Awareness has also spoken of using your own BS meter to feel out the events and circumstances that are happening on the planet, but also then that are happening in your own personal life. One of the most important elements of having a good and strong BS meter is the use of common sense. Unfortunately, as the saying goes, common sense is often not too common.

And it would seem often that when you have an alternative view of things and you try to speak to others about these views, about this information, they will not be responsive to you, mostly because they are not using their own common sense to ask questions, logical questions, questions of importance that often are not even looked at. And any ones holding such a common-sense point of view are often degraded and put down as conspiracy theorists, of course a term that was introduced by the CIA after the John F. Kennedy coup d'état. And this is still the major way that those who would malign you, those who would put you down, those who would deny you, still respond that it is all conspiracy theory, it is all nonsense. But they do not use their own common sense, often, to look at the situations and to ask the critical questions.

Therefore this Awareness does remind all to always come from the place of common sense. The questions you ask do not necessarily have to have answers. But by putting those questions out there, those common-sense questions, you have a better handle on things. You will be able to understand something that does not make sense, is something that must be suspect, and you can then always look at alternatives. You can be creative then in how you respond to the series of events that are being presented, how they are being interpreted by others who are not asking common-sense questions.

The shooting in Florida is an example of this. How it is that the masses are told to not pay any attention to information that is contradictory to the events that are being given you, that are being played out for you, that are being suggested to you through the mainstream media for example. For an example, do not ask the common-sense questions of how it is that a young woman can say she was with the shooter at a time when the shots were ringing out. And this young man was not in body armor, did not have a weapon in his hand, and they both did not understand what was happening.

Those who present such information are put down. It is denied by the mainstream media which has their own agenda. And this false flag event is certainly being manufactured and controlled so an outcome can be reached that is to their liking, because it is part of the solution they have already formulated, part of that which they wish to create. This is but one example of how common sense is being trumped in a way that makes no sense. And that when you listen to alternative presentations of the truth of the day, your common sense will certainly guide you to the conclusions that actually are the truth behind the lies. This is that which occurs on many levels.

This is but one example of how to use your own common sense when false flag events happen, so that immediately right from the beginning, you are aware this is a false flag event. And those behind it have an agenda, are using these false flags as a way of moving the masses forward, moving the sheeple towards the holding pens where they are trying to direct humanity.

But luckily this Awareness can say they are not as effective as they have been in the past. For the energies that are now playing out are not only the energies of manipulation, but rather that which is Divine Source itself, Spirit itself, that is now coming through stronger and stronger each and every day.

This Awareness of course is aware that to the many who are having the earthly experience, the matter of time seems to be a very strong factor in everything, because time does not seem to be showing much change. That is why many say nothing is happening, when so much is happening.

Of course if one is coming from a position where the belief system is based on outside events, outside reporting of events, the mass media, mainstream media for example, it may well seem that nothing is happening. But as one shifts the focus, as one starts to understand how to go within oneself to feel out the news, to ask the common-sense questions, to be open to alternatives, then the answers that are relevant to you on a personal level will come through.

It does still at this stage take an act of faith and trust that things certainly are not as they seem. And as one digs a little and holds a different attitude, the truth will be felt out, will be presented. Your BS meters will be effective in cutting through the bullshit and coming to the clarity that lies beyond the surrounding information that is released for the masses.

This therefore is a very exciting time in human history, and by extension, in your own personal histories. And because it is so that it is exciting, it can also sometimes be quite challenging. But to hold that the challenges, which is part of the growth and development, the clearing the way of the obstruction, the dwelling into the heart of the matter, the essence of the information and the energies, that this is a way forward for all. Especially when this is a catfight of extreme importance. Especially when those who have had control for so long are becoming more and more desperate in their actions and their opinions.

Remember that an animal cornered is the most dangerous of all. And those who have had power for so long are in the corner and are desperate. On one level this will make many of their actions very obvious to those who have opened their minds and their hearts. But at the same time please be aware that there are many who do not recognize this, do not understand this.

And your role, if you will, is to have patience with the many who are not seeing things clearly, where you can speak of such things. But if there is resistance, if there is anger, if there is an attack upon you, do not proceed to explain to one who will not listen and does not wish to know.

Be open to the many who are starting to awaken, who are asking questions. They will see your light. They will understand, "Here is one that might give me some information." And when those who are seeking come to you, those would be the ones indeed to explain matters to. And if you find this is not so in your own personal situation, that people are not speaking to you, or there is not the opportunity to explain this to others, then simply hold the space. Or as the crypto-currency phrase goes, HODL, HODL, hang on for dear life and hold the energies.

Know this shift is happening. You are part of the shift and that shift is of an extreme quality at this time. Know that even if you are not one who speaks to others, you are still very important in the equation of the energies that are playing out at this time. Because for each who holds a new level of comprehension, for each who understands the truth is not always what it seems to be as presented by those who have vested interests, that this too is of great importance, you are of great importance.

At the same time as you work this within yourself, as you see how it affects you in a personal way, the freedom you will find will be immense. Know also this is still part of a longer agenda that is being carried on. It is not as it is on the level from which this Awareness, speaks something that is necessarily instantaneous in terms of human timing and the human experience of time. Everything is still in slow motion.

It takes a while for things to seemingly work out but if one can hold on, can HODL, and in these times can focus their attention to themselves, their own growth, their own shift, their own ability to go beyond that which is the container that you have been placed in, that humanity has been placed in, then you will indeed see how things are getting clearer, how things are shifting and changing, even if this does not seem to be reflected through your mainstream media or through the many that surround you, be they friends, family or other.

Garden Meditation

This Awareness would ask all, right now in this moment, to visualize yourselves coming to gather in the garden, to see yourselves coming together as a circle of ones who are here to look deeper, to have an experience beyond the norm.

Now, seeing that ball of light descending from above, and that it settles in a position in the middle of your circle. Feel the energy of this ball of light. Feel the energy in the circle. Feel your own energies aligning now with this ball of light.

This Awareness asks you now to shift your consciousness. You are still around the ball, but now the ball of light is the Central Sun of Mother Earth, and you are all in the space in the center of the planet herself. And that you are seeing her beating heart, her illumination.

You are there. You are part of her illumination, part of the fabric of consciousness that she constitutes that she is.

Now see the group going into the light, into the pulsing light, to the heart of Mother Earth. There is no heat, there is no discomfort. There is the expansion into the consciousness of Mother Earth who herself is part of the consciousness of the cosmos, part of that which is the Divine Source that is this Awareness.

Know that you are contained lovingly in the energies of Divine Source and in the heart of Mother Earth.

And it is so.

Death, Resurrection, and Common Sense

Without the ending of what once was,
no new beginning can happen,
no re-birth will take place —

That indeed this Awareness does have a public message at this time, for these times. It is the long weekend, the festival of the Christian faith that is known as Easter. And while it is that many are not Christians, still there is an energetic involved in this religious weekend that has significance for all. This Awareness is not identifying the Easter weekend as that which is critical to all, suggesting all should follow the Christian lead on this matter. It is simply saying there are principles involved in that which is known as Easter, including Good Friday and Easter Sunday, that have importance in the human experience. This is a universal that can apply to all faiths, not subscribing to any one faith as the true faith, but all contributing to that which is the human experience. And so it is that this Easter celebration of the Christian faith has significance universally for all humans.

This Awareness would take this discussion first to the day known as Good Friday, the day of the crucifixion of the one known as Jesus Christ. And to the Christian faith this is a powerful day, a sad day, but also a day that represents for them that which was the extinguishing of the life of the one that has become for many of the Christian faith the single most important person of the Trinity. This of course again being the one known as Jesus Christ.

The death of Jesus Christ on the day known as Good Friday is the first day of the weekend towards the resurrection on the Sunday, Easter Sunday. First, in terms of Good Friday the theme if you will, is about death, the dying on the cross for the many who were to become Christians, or so this is taught. But the truth, the universal truth here is that all things come to an end. All things come to that point of death where there is release. Many do not understand this. Many are frightened of the concept of death. Even the word death has a powerful negative connotation for many, but without the ending of what once was, no new beginning can happen, no re-birth will take place.

Looking at this concept, the concept of endings, the concept of death, Good Friday represents if you will, a very powerful concept, the universal concept that there must be endings so new beginnings can occur, so resurrection can take place. In terms of world events at this time there is an energy, a strong energy of endings taking place. The death experience is very evident at this time not only in terms of the horrendous wars that are occurring and are taking place on the planet at this time which cause the physical death of many, but also the death of the concepts and beliefs held by so many for so long.

In the United States of America at this time there is great turbulence as that which has been a way of living is coming to an end. It has not ended. It is a process still playing out but this Awareness would say that the country of the United States of America, and the Americans, are going through this very strong death experience with their politics, with their beliefs of the rights of the American citizen, the regaining of those rights.

What is coming to a death, what is unravelling, is the control that has been exerted not only on the United States but globally as well. But in particular in America there is a movement to displace and replace the corrupted government's leadership and authorities that have had power for so long. And many are frightened of this, many are resistant of this.

This Awareness would remind all once again that the death experience makes it possible to move on, to re-birth that which is no longer valid, to bring new life, new understanding, new beliefs, new freedom into the scope of things, into the scape, the landscape of that which has been a way of life for many for so long. Moving this theme forward to the day of resurrection and rebirth, that it is believed by the Christian faith, that Jesus the Lord was resurrected on the day now known as Easter Sunday, and this is the most powerful and strongest message of the Christian faith.

But it is again a universal truth that there will be always the resurrection from that which was the conclusion of one way of life, to be born into a new state of consciousness, a new reality. Therefore, symbolically Easter Sunday does represent the universal truth that there will be rebirth, there will be resurrection, not only in the way offered by the Christian faith or other faiths that hold similar concepts, but in the way of the universal truth that all will be reborn into the higher state of their own conscious being.

There is the resurrection of a state, a state governed by principles that are coming to an end. And therefore the universal symbology of Easter, that there is resurrection after the ending of things, is appropriate in the viewing of the energies taking place at this time in America. These energies are quite troubled; these energies are very challenging. These energies are of a nature that there are those who believe and there are those who oppose.

It can be seen at this time that there is a group of ones who are now starting to question the authenticity and the appropriateness of ones who are corrupted, to be the leaders. There is the exposure of information against many who have had power and control for so long, and this is a very challenging matter. There is also a situation taking place at this very time amongst those very ones who are searching deeply into the history of events, into the validity of power and the power elites. The movement, the freedom movement, the patriot movement if you will, is being divided in itself, amongst itself.

Those who are in power are at this time very much in their desperation, creating situations of conflict amongst the ones who would oppose those who have had power for so long. It is an age-old tactic, the tactic of divide and conquer. For those in power are desperate to maintain their power, maintain their agenda. For there is a long agenda here that has been planned out not for dozens of years but for hundreds of years; that is in threat now of being exposed, of being eliminated. This too is the movement towards a rebirth, a new way of knowing, of understanding, of being. But on a practical level part of the desperate response, as it has always been, is to divide and conquer that group that have come together in recent times, who have been asking deep and powerful questions at this time. This is a situation that could have detrimental effect if you allow it to have.

This Awareness advises all who are indeed caught up in this internalized struggle, this divide and conquer, to understand this is a necessity at this time to define the borders and boundaries of a movement that has just begun. Common sense must be used to view the events, the circumstances of events, that are unfolding at this time. This divide and conquer can be seen through if one holds common sense as that which guides one through this situation presenting itself at this time.

Also it is necessary not to become too attached to the outcome. By this, this Awareness means that if you hold to something as that which is of the greatest importance, then your life will reflect this; your personal lives will reflect this.

That as you become more neutral in observing the events that are coming, as you develop patience to see things through, and as you hold within yourself that which you wish for, which is your preference, the events will begin to alter to support your own personal belief system and way of being. This is an important concept especially during challenging times, for it is only too easy to forget common sense and to be swayed emotionally by the arguments presented by this side or that side, even within the patriot movement, even within one's own nation.

That as you stay neutral, as you are the observer, as you do not attach to the outcome but hold within yourself that which is desired by you as the way of things, the way you would see things unfold, you will find this does become your own personal reality. As you understand these concepts you step more into your own personal power and find within yourself the freedom guaranteed by the Constitution. And you will begin to recognize that this freedom is your birth right, is the Divine Right given to you as spiritual beings by that source that is Divine Source Itself.

Therefore during the weekend and beyond, remember there is always the ending of things so something new can be born. It is a matter of choice as to what you would prefer to see in your life. If you believe those who are giving you information that is false, because you are not questioning, you are not delving deeper into the truth of things, then it may be that you need this experience.

But if you are willing to ask questions, to look deeply, to hold that neutral space, to be the observer in the center of your circle, you will be shown through the unfolding events, that which will improve your life, that which will bring to you the historical developments that have been underway for quite some time which are coming to a head at this time.

It is the way forward, it is a way of dealing with challenging times, that will indeed give you personal freedom and liberty, and bring to you a sense of your own being and your own power as a divine spark of Divine Source Itself.

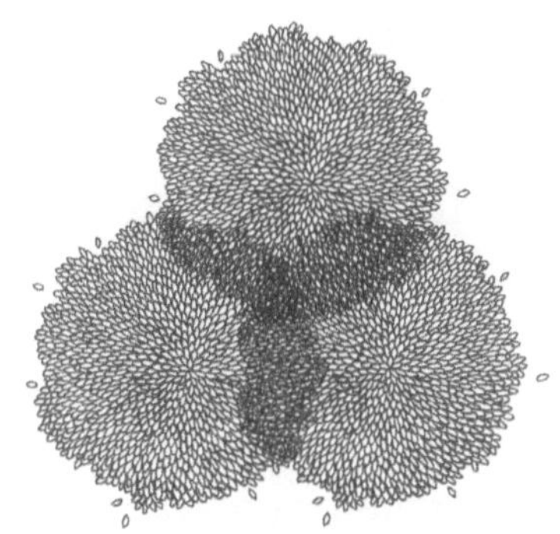

The Force Behind the Scene

As you tie in to your own high level experience in consciousness, you will understand the contexts of events —

That which is Cosmic Awareness greets one and all. It greets you at this most monumental of times, this most pressing of times, this most historical of times. It asks you to remember you have all chosen to be here now, to be part of these historical times, to be part of the energies that are percolating at this very moment.

Some of those energies are very strong and seemingly are very negative in nature. Others are of a more uplifting variety, and can indeed serve you and lift you to new realms of your own perception and your own experiences. Experiences that are based not on your singularity as the third dimensional being restricted and limited, but rather as a multi-dimensional being that has at the same moment other elements, other aspects of your own consciousness that are very active and are playing a part in these times, both here on this planet, but beyond the realms of the physical, beyond the realms of this planet.

As the events play themselves out, do not get stuck into the negative fear and anger and frustration, of actions that on the surface seem detrimental and indeed even evil in their content and in their expression. Do not worry so much that there has been a strike on Syria by three nations. But see rather that there are communications taking place behind the scenes, unknown by you because they are not reported on. There are conversations between America and Russia for example, and while they play out their roles for the benefit of the mass media, the controlled media, it does not mean there is not a game plan behind the actions that are taken and are taking place.

Many felt that if a strike on Syria occurred it could be preliminary to an escalation of hostilities leading to another world war, the third World War. While there are timelines that may contain such events, you are not involved in those timelines unless you are so caught up by them, so believing of them that you put your focus there and hence your energies. But this Awareness assures you all, that as seen from the perspective of this Awareness, none of you are actually as involved in that negative framework as you might think. It does not mean you are not feeling the effects of a disruption in the force of consciousness that is the collective of humanity.

Many of you are feeling it very personally and in that personal experience there is indeed the element of fear, of sadness, of sorrow, of grieving for actions that are less than enlightened. But if you remember always there are those behind the scenes. And this is not even saying those actors behind the scenes, but it is a reference directly now to the force in consciousness that is Divine Source, that is Spirit, that is you and your expansion in consciousness to levels much beyond the levels of the personal experience. And as you tie in to your own high level experience in consciousness, you will understand the contexts of events that are occurring are in accordance to these bigger plans, to the big game being played out not only in the physical but also in the spiritual levels.

There is an adjustment coming about now, and for that adjustment to take place, actions do need to be taken that in a limited way are seemingly very detrimental to the human experience. But if you also remember that those who have had power for so long are now in a situation of complete desperation. And they are even doing criminal actions in order to try to pull it back for themselves, but they have already been defeated. And the future is known to be a future where these ones no longer have power or control. And humanity has come through these moments that seem to be so challenging and negative at this time.

Look beyond the moment, in that you are able to project your consciousness into the future, into your future, into the future of humanity. And hold that this is indeed that very time you have chosen to be involved in, to be part of. And how it is, that as you are part of the greater collective in consciousness that goes well beyond even the collective of humanity, it is the intent and purpose of that collective you are part of, that Divine Source energies that all are part of, that are also very much at play here and behind the scene.

If you have the experience that you are exhausted, or you are spinning, or you are feeling grief and sadness, take the moment to simply release this, to let it go, to say to yourself that it is all right, that there are ones involved, the Divine Source itself is involved. And that which is playing itself out, while distressing on some levels, is part of the bigger picture as well. And the actions taken by those few will come back at them one way or another, or will open new portals, new doorways of understanding and awareness as those who are the corrupt ones are exposed more and more, and their lies and their deceit are exposed for all to see.

It is a struggle that this Awareness can say in the framework of the physical experience[s] are monumental indeed, and yet they are very much contained within the fabric of the Divine orchestration of the energies. And this comes from beyond the experience in the physical. As you identify not with the limited and restricted being you may think yourself to be in the physical, and identify more with your expanded consciousness, and the understanding that you are an aspect of the Divine Source expressing itself at this time. And you are part of the energies of the Divine Source in these times.

You may well understand that everything happening is but an illusion. And it is only when you energize it without this balance, without this neutrality, the sacred neutrality, that you are most affected. Look around and see how many are affected because they are not in their neutrality, in their balance, in their centeredness. Know that they are going through what is necessary for them to come to a new realization and understanding of things. Know that they are coming through a shift in consciousness that they do not understand.

And therefore, for many the journey may be a rough journey. But do not identify with their problems, their focus, with their intent, rather go beyond it. As this Awareness has just said, find the centeredness of your being and expand out from it. Call to those higher levels of your own consciousness, those parts of yourself that are multi-dimensional and lie beyond the framework of the reality of experience that you the focus personality is going through at this time.

Remember also that while many are afraid of death, that death itself is an illusion and not simply the snuffing of the experience of life, but rather the transition from one state of consciousness to another. Many are afraid of death because they think they will be eradicated, erased, removed from consciousness, when nothing could be further from the truth.

It is that time of expansion into the greater framework of your own reality of Spirit, and this reality of Spirit supersedes the illusional state that you are experiencing at this moment. If you understand death is nothing but that moment of transition, then perhaps you can lose the fear of death that so many have, that so many feel so abject about, so distraught about, so fearful of. And as you move through the levels of consciousness in your own personal experience, calling in your higher states of consciousness, you will begin to understand, but even more importantly you will begin to feel the complexity of your own spiritual nature. And how it is important to have focus, but it is also important to go beyond focus.

As you deal with such matters you will also begin to understand many experience in life a fear of life itself, a fear of the experience of life. For as they see it from that negative perspective where things are happening to them, they are afraid then of change. They are afraid to let it go, to look at things differently, to understand in the nature of the shift in consciousness, that this actually means many things that were once known and held to be so are coming to an end, are coming to the death of the experience.

But as already mentioned, the death experience itself is but transition, whether it is the death of the body and transition back into spirit, or the death of the precepts and concepts that have held humans down, held them back. This including the nature of reality regarding nation-states, the political experiences that have been experienced over the decades and centuries, the limitation of the physical body, its capacity not to be able to heal itself for example. And this is all part of the shifting in consciousness happening now.

Therefore, welcome life. Welcome the experience you are having in the life you are involved in right now. Know that you are truly ascended beings who have come back into a reality form, a body, to have these experiences and to be part of the changes that are happening, the transition that is occurring, the endings that are taking place. For this is as it is, and it is as you choose it to be.

That life itself is a wondrous experience if you hold it is so. These are not necessarily evil times but rather exciting times, the times of endings and new beginnings, the time of transition from the old mindset of reality to something so new that it can hardly be imagined. Remember, as you have chosen to be here, you have also chosen then to remember how it is beyond the precepts and concepts that have hemmed humanity in for so long. You know it within yourself, you hold it within yourself.

Be joyous in that you are here as part of the solution, not simply part of the problem. And as those who are here promoting the problem, the evil, the dark mindsets, are seen and comprehended, you will take away from them their capacity to be in charge. This is already occurring. This is part of that which this Awareness calls the big plan, the big game. And this is a game that has ramifications of a most positive nature, even though to get there you must go through the disruptions that you experience from time to time, great disruptions like that which was experienced on 13 April [2018], great disruptions in the collective force of consciousness of humanity.

When you are going through these experiences, remember always that while you may be experiencing it on a personal level, it is within your right to simply sleep through it, to relax through it, to release from it and to let it all play out while holding, holding, holding that all will be fine. For that is in accordance to the Divine purpose and nature of Divine Source Itself.

And you are part of Divine Source. You are a spark of the Goddess and God, and that which is the highest level of Divine Spirit Itself. And it is so.

Heading Into A Storm

America is about to go into a violent storm of reaction and action —

Several months ago, at the beginning of the year, this Awareness put a public message out, the title along the lines of the "message for the week ahead" or some version of this. At that time this Awareness was speaking of the year ahead, not only the week ahead, as being a time where the energies that had been released during the summer, especially with the solar eclipse throughout the United States, as being an energy that was releasing, unzippering even, that which is the United States of America to allow certain energies to finally be released.

In January It [Awareness] continued more or less with the theme that the energies were very intense and would be so for the rest of the year. Now, halfway through the year, this Awareness is pointing out yet again how the energies, which have been released for several months, that are exposing the underbelly of the beast that has been in control for so long, have continued to build up.

Recently, a picture through the White House agencies has been released of the White House with storm clouds gathering and this was simply put out without comment. But this Awareness would make comment. For this image takes that which this Awareness has spoken of over the last several months, and indeed in the public message in January, as those energies that are building up and building up. The picture showing the White House is seen to have these built-up clouds, these storm clouds, over it. The White House presented is also symbolic of America and that there are storms gathering in the skies above America.

This Awareness would say, be prepared! For there have been events recently that have come to light that are a breach in the dam that has contained the knowledge, the information, the truth of what has been so in America for so long. The hidden corruption of ones in power, and what they have done with their power, and how they have used it to serve themselves and their agenda, their New World order, their globalist agenda.

These ones in power are being exposed but they are not without the capacity to strike back. And it is seen that with the release of recent information, especially information regarding a camp found in the Tucson area that seems to have been a holding place for children and part of an underground network of tunnels throughout the South West, but even throughout all of the United States. This has simply not been recognized or understood previously, but now this information has come out and it is causing a reaction amongst those whose secrets are starting to be revealed.

The image of the White House under the storm clouds is suggesting that America is about to go into a violent storm of reaction and actions. The ones who have their secrets being revealed are seen to be ones who are trying to squash things, to crush things, to bring things to a halt, this tying into the ongoing situation in America where those who were opponents to Trump because they are being exposed, are getting desperate in their actions of opposition. Their lies, their claims against Trump becoming more and more extreme. This is also part of the attack on the White House.

But what this Awareness is simply pointing out here is that the storm is unleashed. It is a storm that will have much bearing upon the truth of the land and for the people that is being revealed. A truth many do not want to hear or acknowledge. Yet the storm is here.

And this Awareness would suggest the best thing is not to be afraid of the storm, but to understand this storm has the potential of cleansing and clearing that which is the corruption of America. It is that which was seen as the unzippering in August coming to a new level, a new accumulation of energies that are in motion now. Energies that will reveal many deep, ugly, dark secrets. Energies that will bring certain ones down, that will challenge the psyche of America and the soul of America. And it is still part of that ongoing energy that this Awareness spoke to in January and in August 2017.

Be prepared. The storm is raging and it is time.

You Are the Awakened Ones

You can exceed the definition of a third dimensional human being

That which is Cosmic Awareness is now available and greets one and all. Most certainly the events over the last few weeks in regards to the [local] weather events have been peculiar and strange. But, they are no more peculiar and strange in that which is occurring in other regions around the planet. Last year, one saw many of these strange unnatural weather events occurring in the United States, in Canada, in Europe, and it is to be understood that there are those who definitely have, as an objective and an agenda, the destruction of great areas, the death of many individuals, for that is still part of a plan that has been put into motion many years ago and that has been planned out for even longer.

But, what is also so, as the discussion shows, is the capacity for spiritual human beings with understanding, intent, and purpose, to stand in the way to block these events, to mute them, to diminish them. This is especially so when it is realized you are in conjunction with that which is Holy Spirit Itself, Divine Source Itself.

That as you align yourself to the Will of the Divine Source, as the voice, as the focus of that intent on this planet in this world, you can direct these energies elsewhere away from localized areas and out of the danger zone. This is part of the discovery of who you really are as sentient spirit beings who are alive on this the third dimensional level at this time, but who exceed that definition of a third dimensional human being, who exceed that which are the physical parameters that are assigned to this third dimensional state of being.

Make no mistake about it, it is a very serious time in terms of those who would destroy, those who would diminish, those who would control. They still think it is their time and they are carrying out their actions with what they think is immunity from any consequence, but they are finding out this is no longer so.

But part of that which is the overall plan is to keep humans dumbed down, to keep them asleep thus ignorant of the truth of their situation, the truth of their being. That truth is that you are spiritual in your nature, in your core. And you have the power and ability to exceed the third dimension, to create from that which this Awareness refers to as the fifth dimensional state of consciousness. But, how do you know this is so? Part of the discussion in regards to the weather situations experienced here and elsewhere, is to help you understand you can actually do this and see the results almost immediately.

But, there are other areas that this Awareness would ask you to look to, in terms of how you as a spirit being are no longer the old ones that were so restricted, the old routine, the old forum of consensus that defines humanity, that defines the physical state. You are the forerunners, you are the way-showers, you are those early pioneers into a whole new realm of being. But how do you know this? As already expressed, certainly you may have the spectacular examples of directing your will, adding your will to the will of others, to the will of the Divine, to direct weather events. But it is not simply weather events that you can direct; you can direct your own life, you can direct that which you call into your life.

The last time this Awareness spoke, it spoke of moving from one state over the border to another state, and at the beginning when you make such a transition it is hard to tell you have arrived in another state. But with time, with the journey going on, with practice, you will begin to understand you no longer are who you once were, what you once were. But you will also understand you are becoming more the one you really are, and have always been.

How do you confirm this? This is a question many ask, for many find it hard to believe they are other than what they were once upon a time. Many find it hard to call into their lives the factors, the proof, the evidence that they think they need to have in order to know that they are different now, they are fifth dimensional.

Also, there are those who think this shift into fifth dimensionality should be instant. It certainly was seen on December 21, 2012 when so many who had anticipated that grand shift, the great instantaneous shift into fifth dimensional consciousness. How it was that for them, for many of them, for many of you, nothing happened. Because the world did not change instantly, did not become this new world. And as a result many were deflated, many were upset. Many broke away from that movement towards the high expression of consciousness at that which is a fifth dimensional state of awareness in the fourth and third dimensional level of participation.

Since then, since that time, the gate has been opened and the energies have been constantly shifting and changing and growing. And there are many events each year where the power of the Divine and the Supreme comes through in new waves. A most recent wave saw the frequencies of all change and shift and many of you were aware of this on some level of your being, some more so than others. But for many it was still not enough and is still not enough, for many want to see the evidence in cold hard facts in front of them, in evidence in front of them.

For example, many hold that their situation is a situation of poverty and struggle and hardship because there is not enough money. And they feel that there is only one answer: to have more money. And if more money was suddenly brought to you for example, if you suddenly won a lottery and won millions of dollars then you could believe. Because now you have the evidence, now you have the cold hard cash in front of you; and because it does not arrive many do not accept, or yet believe, that they are manifesting on a much higher level than they have ever manifested before.

This Awareness says however, what is abundance? If you call money into your life, it is not that you cannot manifest money but many have very negative concepts and beliefs regarding money. There are many who at the subconscious and lower self level, do not accept having money. For there are many beliefs, core beliefs, old programs, that are happening in the subconscious, that would sabotage the manifestation of money, because money is evil, money corrupts, money is the vice of those who are the greedy ones, the dark ones.

If any of these beliefs and others are there in the subconscious, never recognized, never worked with, never deleted, if the old program continues on and on and on, even though at that level of intellectual comprehension you may think that you should be able to call money into your life as you are, after all, magical Creator beings. But, in the subconscious you have any level of objection, any program running, any core beliefs held against money, against having such wealth, then this Awareness guarantees you, you will not call money into your life. The evidence that you say you want will be denied you, because you do not believe you can manifest this money.

But, if you hold instead an attitude of abundance, and you hold that abundance flows to you, not qualifying it only as money but abundance on all levels, certainly financial abundance will be there in the monies you need for your life will be there. But so will physical abundance in such matters as health, and perhaps friends or community, or all manner of things that are abundance in action.

Happiness, Enjoyment, Pleasure. This is all that which is also part of abundance in your life. And as you find that, you also find the lightning of your life as it lightens up, as the light flows in.

What is important in all of this, is you do the work that this Awareness has spoken of many, many times over. And what is this work then? It is the work on oneself, it is the digging deep into one's own being to see why it is that the very things you think are possible never happen to you, never manifest in your life and, your life still is a struggle. It is still fraught with negativity; unrecognized, unknown, not taken on board.

By this, this Awareness means you do not take it on board in a conscious way where you have examined what it is that is blocking you, is sabotaging you. You have not opened to the low self, you have not worked with that level of your multi-dimensional being that is the gate into this physical reality and that draws into your life, that which are the concepts and precepts, that which is the actuality of your life.

You do not see the negative programs that are running because they are so subtle and so deeply buried, that you simply do not understand at some level that this is what is happening, and this is what is preventing you from seeing the evidence you ask for. The subtlety of evidence that is presented is sometimes not acknowledged or recognized.

Therefore, this Awareness is calling to you all to begin to harvest that within yourself that is your true capacity, and your true calling. And not to simply deny it, or believe otherwise, as you are Creator beings and as you create from the level of your imagination and your ability to image or imagine, that which you can call into your life, that which you can experience.

If you do not deal with those restrictions, those blocks, those barriers, those misguided beliefs, then they will continue to have effect on you. The low self will continue to manifest, for part of its need of you, the middle self, you the conscious one, is direction. And to help the low self deal with those issues, to let the low self understand it is not abandoned any longer, it is not left in the dark room deep underground alone. To manifest what it is told, it should manifest the programs that run the low self, are not challenged by the middle self, by you. The high self is there for you as well, to guide you, to help you understand the capacity you have as a fifth dimensional being.

But, if you do not take responsibility for yourselves and you simply think that it should change for you, because you want it to change, this is not enough. You must look much deeper into that which is that well-pool, that well-spring of your own being, that is the low self that is waiting to be guided and directed. Waiting for the parent to hold his/her hand, and to walk out of the darkness. This too is part of the evolution of the spirit of humanity and the spirit of the individual. And as you move into a greater comprehension of who and what you really are, and as you call forth those high spiritual powers and energies that are there for you, are there with you, and as you claim the royalty of your own being, that which is your right to be the creator being becomes stronger and stronger.

It is always and has always been your right, but as it has always been controlled that which is your capacity to create consciously, with intent and purpose. There has been then, the situation you are now coming out of but are still very much involved in. This being the situation of being ineffective human beings, who are victims, who cannot change their lives, who must endure the grapes of wrath that are thrown at them, that are experienced by them, because this is how it is. This is the belief so many still have. But you are all not those ones who were once controlled and manipulated, and who are still controlled and manipulated by the few who have an understanding of how it really works.

You are the awakened ones. You are the fifth dimensional ones who are here now, to awaken even further to the power of your being, to the alignment with Spirit, and to the discovery that you are most definitely and truly Creator beings. This Awareness over the last months has spoken to how there has been an unzippering in America, but globally as well, and that there is that which is the darkness that is coming out. The putridness that has been contained is being released, more and more at this time. But, you do not simply have to have this wash over you. You can see what is happening and call into the effect that which is the higher state of being, which is also coming at this very time onto the planet and into the psyche of humanity. And as you work on yourself, as you work with your low self, your capacity to be effective become stronger and stronger, clearer and clearer.

This is all which you are here to accomplish and achieve, if it is your desire, intent, and will, to do so. But this is also part of your responsibility in that nobody will simply give it to you. Divine Source is not here to instantly change this reality into a fifth dimensional state, but it is here to support the evolution towards that state of consciousness and that state of being. And, it all starts with you, each of you, as individuals who are aligned with their inner strength and power of Divine Source Itself, with this Cosmic Awareness, with the collective nature of your own being as it exhibits itself in the higher dimensions full and complete. In respect to that which is the high self, the middle self, and the low self, this is the expression of your multi-dimensionality at the most personal level.

The low self, that which is the subconscious, can be seen to be the unevolved level of consciousness that has not yet stepped into a level of awareness.

The middle self is that level of consciousness that has begun the journey, that has awareness and understanding but still needs to differentiate between the reality of the third dimensional alleged 'real world' versus the real world of the Divine source that you are part of.

And then there is the high self that is the advancement of that which has been the soul's journey as it has expressed itself in higher consciousness and it is ready to guide the middle self and support the low self in the evolutionary process of oneself into realization of the wholeness and completeness that you truly and completely are.

You are spirit beings having this life by intent, and with intent, you have the capacity to create consciously, or unconsciously. You have a responsibility, but it is also the privilege, to awaken to the truth of who and what you really are. And these are the times now in which to do this.

You Are the Awakened Ones. It is your calling. It is your purpose. It is your intent. And it is aligned with the intent, calling, and purpose of the Divine Source of the Everything and the All.

You Are No Longer in Kansas

You are now in a different reality set

This Awareness has spoken of the fact that you are now in a different reality set. It has given the example of coming to a boundary, a border of one state into another, one country into another, and how it is that once you've crossed that defining line that is invisible in nature, it is hard to tell you are in another state, another country.

So it is at this time. As that which is occurring is of a nature that it is progressive and continual, but you do not necessarily see the results when you have shifted from one state of consciousness, to another state of consciousness that is now the defining state of your consciousness. This Awareness declares that you are fifth dimensional in your nature. And yet many do not recognize this or understand it, especially as they view their reality as the reality they have always known. This would be the third dimensional reality.

So how is it that a fifth dimensional being can actually see or understand that they are no longer in Kansas? that they have shifted their state of consciousness, and now have access to that which is a higher state of consciousness - higher only in the sense that it is beyond the third dimensional reality set?

Now is the time for you to understand you have shifted, and you are no longer truly subject to third dimensional rules and laws exclusively. Certainly it is that while you are in a third dimensional state, there are those laws of third dimensionality that apply. They apply only because you still believe in them: these laws, these rules, these definitions of reality that define the third dimensional state of consciousness.

If you do not know that you actually exceed third dimensionality, and even that which is fourth dimensionality, then it is only natural you will continue to play in that arena of third dimensionality, expecting things to exhibit themselves in the same way they have always exhibited themselves. Thus it is so, that even if you are of a fifth dimensional nature,as long as you hold to your third dimensionality, or you define yourself in accordance to the rules and laws of their dimensionality, it will be very difficult to ever realize you are in a different state now, and you can do things differently now.

Those who own animals especially of a domestic nature that wander the pastures and paddocks, may have the experience of containing that group of animals within a certain parameter, and this is often done with the use of an electrical fence, a fence that will deliver a shock if an animal tries to go through that electrified fence. At first the shock is of a nature that the animal will repel from that fence, but it may well try again, maybe even several times before the message becomes loud and clear to the animal that to approach this fence, to touch this fence will bring forth an unpleasant experience.

When this is definitely within the context of understanding for that animal or creature, then it is unlikely they will approach the fence again, once they have equated that fence with the electrical shock they will receive. Thus all a farmer needs to do then is to put up the fence but not necessarily turn it on. For the animal was so convinced that to touch that fence, to go beyond that fence would be painful and therefore they do not try any longer to exceed the boundaries that have been set up around them.

What if it is so that, in your perception of reality, you are in the same situation as a creature is that is contained within the electrified area that is defined by the fence itself? What if this electrified fence is the definition of third dimensionality? And how it is that you have had enough experiences with the physical third dimensional reality to know where you are limited by it, where you cannot exceed it, where you must play the rules of the game because you are set in context to that game, in that you are contained within that game and within the boundaries and borders of that which defines that area or that mindset.

Therefore many will not try to exceed themselves, will not try to create a new reality that exceeds a limited reality. For they believe still, and it may be so that you believe still, that you cannot call into your life those other levels of reality that exceed a third dimensional mindset. And like the creatures contained within the electrified fence, you are content to stay within the parameters defining your experience in accordance to the space you are in. However, as fifth dimensional beings you have the capacity to exceed the fence, to exceed the restraints that confine you, but you must do this with intent and purpose, with belief that this is so.

Remember also you are working with the low self, and the low self is that which has put up the fence in accordance to the belief structure that your low self holds. And if it is so that the low self believes in a physical reality and constructs your experience of that reality to always reflect a third dimensional state of being, then it is unlikely that the third dimensional barriers will be breached by a subconscious that does not believe it has the capacity to do this. It is that which has been programmed, and in the running of the program is that which is the constraining boundary or barrier of beliefs that indeed keep you locked up and contained within a mindset of third dimensionality.

But these are different times now. And this Awareness has said already you are no longer in Kansas. You have already crossed the boundary line, a border. And in this new reality, even though it is not immediately perceived that you are in this new reality, so it is nonetheless. This then requires a new mindset, a new set of experiences as you begin to see in your own experiencing of reality, the reality you are part of, different results occurring.

One of the biggest constraints to the experience one has in terms of their own freedom as creator beings, is the constraint that has been imposed due to the mindset, the assumptions, the beliefs and programming of abundance in one's life. That you have been taught right from the cradle onward, that you cannot have anything if you cannot pay for it, if you do not have enough money for it.

And thus it is that humans are taught to continually strive for things in this physical reality in accordance to how it should be. And how it is, that you must work hard, have a job, have money coming in, in order to buy things, in order to afford a life of luxury which most do not have because the mindset is not a mindset of abundance, but rather a mindset of scarcity and poverty.

Thus most believe in the poverty of oneself and from this perspective treat their lives as that which is confined and constrained to a poverty mentality, where you do not have enough, where you must strive and work hard to receive anything. You cannot simply wish it into your life, for this is not applicable in a third dimensional mindset. Effort must be made, physical effort. There must be sacrifice, there must be pain, there must be suffering, in order to attain enough money, which is the definition of the physical reality of how one can afford the things one wishes for. And not simply the much more liberated way of doing it, which is simply to wish for it, to put out one's intent, to work with the low self and the high self, in calling this into your life.

Thus in the programming of one's mind and of one's life, unless one works hard, make sacrifices, one is not entitled to abundance. This is the only way one draws abundance in, and if one works it successfully then they will have money to buy the house, to pay for the car, to have the items one wishes to have in one's life. This is the old way. This is the third dimensional way.

But if you are now fifth dimensional beings living in a third dimensional reality without understanding, you are constrained by old mindsets, old parameters of belief. You will continue to live it this way, just as those creatures confined in an area defined by the electric fence will always stay within the context of that, not even approaching the boundary. But the boundary is no longer turned on. The flow of that which would define the capacity of one to create in their reality has been expanded. And it is now time for you to begin to play in that arena of your own creativity that is the example of fifth dimensional reality.

Thus in the example given about abundance, you do not worry about whether you have made enough money this week, or if you will have enough money when you retire. You simply hold that you are in abundance, that you are like a magnet that attracts abundance to you, and this will become the new reality. Imagine if you will, for imagination is a big part of this new way of being, that you can receive what is needed when you need it. You can receive your wish and your desire if you hold it to be so.

The problem with the old programming of course, is it leaves a residual of disbelief that this can be so. And so you continually look into your third dimensional nature for validation of this new state of being. And when you have a disqualifying belief, a sabotaging belief held at the level of the low self or subconscious, it is more likely you will not see this exemplify itself, present itself in this third dimensional reality.

And then as most do it, the proclamation goes out, "Nothing happened, nothing is happening." And by conjecture and projection, "Nothing ever will happen because it does not work." You can see how this is in itself a type of defining belief system that prevents you from exceeding yourself.

Perhaps what is really needed here is a new attitude towards this matter. And not simply to look out at third dimensionality as the substantial prover of a new reality, but simply one state of being that you have actually surpassed. And in playing with it by putting out that "I am abundance, I live with great wealth, I live within the context of creating what I need when I project it, when I hold it, when I intend it." And rather than to simply stand there awaiting the results in a third dimensional reality, you simply hold it to be so and wait for it to arrive.

That which is a confining belief, is that you must work for something, you must make it happen, you cannot simply wait. You cannot simply put out and allow it to come to you, it must be achieved by your efforts. But what if those efforts now involve the marshaling of your will power, the alignment with your low self and high self to create a new reality for yourself?

What if it is, that while maintaining you are abundance, abundance flows to you, it happens to you? Perhaps not in the way you are told it should happen by working hard, acquiring wealth, acquiring money and then buying things. But it can simply arrive to you in whatever shape or form that is needed by you. This might sometimes be bringing extra cash or money into your life. But it might arrive in other ways as well.

What if you need a new car, and the old way was to think certainly you must work for it, then you must get a loan, then you must pay off the loan before that vehicle is yours. But what if you put out, "I have need of a new automobile, a new car; I hold that a new car will come into my life." And what if someone showed up in your life and said, "I have a vehicle that I no longer need, would you like it?" This would be certainly an accomplishment at that fifth dimensional level of calling into your life something you needed, without that which is the traditional perception of how it is to be done through hard work and effort.

And when you have such an experience, it then reinforces a new way of thinking, a new way of being in your life, towards how you are as a creator being, what it means to put it out there to the universe, to the Divine Source, to your own high self, low self, and allow it come to you. A playful attitude where you are not too immersed in the negativity of, "What if it does not arrive?"; where it can manifest in this new way, is needed here.

Thus it is, you will now understand that you have this capacity, because you begin to experience it. You begin to experience the magic of fifth dimensional reality exemplifying itself in a third dimensional state of being. And this is how you will begin to understand yourself as a fifth dimensional being.

There is also another matter this Awareness would introduce here, and that is the matter of synchronicity. Many think synchronicity is simply the display of digital numbers or the noticing of numbers of significance such as 1111 or 333. There are a number of different number sets that when seen, give one the feeling that this is significant, and it is labeled under that term synchronicity.

But what if synchronicity also involves confirmation of when what you are experiencing, what you are thinking, what you are intending, is valid. For example, one could have an experience where they, the individual, yourself, have experienced something so unusual that it makes you question things. And you wonder if this is a valid thought or a valid experience. And then, as you turn on the radio, perhaps a song that has always had great relevancy is playing or comes on. This would be a confirmation that you are in alignment with whatever it is you have just experienced. If you are not used to this, at first such an experience may be disqualified. At first there will not be trust that this song playing at this exact moment is confirmation of my intent and my desire and my wish.

This is rather strange, this whole experience of a song coming on that has great bearing, great relevancy to you just after you've had the experience, just after you have made a wish or put out your intent. But you will begin to realize that synchronicity is actually more than just significant numbers. It is a way of communicating with the reality of your own being that far exceeds third dimensionality. It is a way that your high self, your spirit self, can communicate to you, can give to you the confirmation of the experience you have had, no matter how unusual. This too is magic. And to live in a reality mindset that looks for magic, that believes in magic, that allows magic, is that which is needed as one moves beyond the parameters and barriers of constraints in one's belief system, or the beliefs of others as well.

Therefore this Awareness says to you all, you are fifth dimensional beings playing in the third dimensional reality. Allow the magic to flow to you. Hold yourself to be that magnet of attraction that allows the magic to flow, to be part of who you are. Not who you were, but who you are now.

This Awareness wishes one and all great joy and happiness, excitement, mirth, and humor as you play in the new arena of your fifth dimensional being.

Shifting Your Reality

Each of you have chosen to be here now —

This Awareness would start by immediately saying that your participation places you in a space of co-operation. Not only for that which is the intent of coming together, but also because there is that energy that is aroused, that is stimulated, that is awoken within each of you as you partake in this gathering, (this gathering of souls who have come together at this time, both in the moment but also in terms of the intent and purpose of the spiritual challenge each of you face), to become more than who you think you are, to open to the greater reality of your being, that which overlooks the intent and purpose of your life.

By that, this Awareness means each of you have chosen to be here now, to be part of a gathering of souls. For as you are all souls, as you are all of spirit, it is so that you have a greater purpose to your intent for being here now, for partaking in the reality you are experiencing, each and every one of you in your own individual way, in your own individual life.

Many of you have the concept that you are greater than that which you have been told you are, but how do you make this the clear and present future you have come here to experience? How do you come into the moment of your being with the fullest understanding you are here now by choice, and that this is not some random event? It is not something you are only speculating on, wondering if there is truth to this, if there is truth to your being of spirit choosing to be here now when it is so difficult it seems, to be in this present reality, this physical reality, that you are all experiencing.

This Awareness says to you all, each and every one of you, the greater reality of your being lies beyond the presentation of the circumstances of life that you are experiencing. By this, this Awareness means there is that which you can access, which you can enter into, that lies beyond the present reality of experience you *are* experiencing.

To reach this point you must become aware of yourselves as spiritual beings. Not simply as words spoken that it is so, but in the actuality of your experience. And to do this you must be willing to let go of certain parameters of belief you have long held, that you have been programmed to believe. One of those parameters, one of those marking points, is that which you are experiencing is the *only* experience there is when this is not true at all. Many of you as dreamers have experiences within the state of dreaming that expand you in your awareness and understanding of your being as that which is of spirit, that which exceeds the parameters of the physical reality. Yet each and every morning you return back into this physical realm, and the knowledge and the knowing that you are more than this, is submerged into the reality of the day, and of the moment you are experiencing.

That this is a time of revelation and discovery. It is a time where imagination can pull you through the constriction of reality that you are each experiencing. In this you will find there are challenges in your life. And the biggest challenge of all is the physical state of being that you find yourself in, quite literally the body that you find yourself in. At this time many of you are experiencing great challenges in the physical, in the state of the body, and the experiences of the body. Many of you are experiencing hardship in the physical realm.

In knowing you are of spirit there is a truth revealed within yourselves that if you bring it to the surface becomes the standing reality of your experience. In this you will find that which is the magical, that which is the miraculous has a place, and becomes a very important part of the waking reality of experience. It is that which you need to look at and to understand is always there, but only when you are able to accept it as the truth of your being and not the illusion you are living in, which in its own way is a trap.

This trap is a very real trap. And herein lies the paradox. How can it be real and unreal at the same time? How can you exceed the parameters of belief that you are experiencing? The way you do this is to go within yourself, to know the core of your being, is the mysterious void, that which is the collection of all consciousness and all experience, of that which is beyond the physical realm of experience.

This will give you a new perspective on your life, a new understanding to how it is that you can be of this physical realm and not be of it. You can see the truth of your own spiritual nature and understand it, but even more importantly to bring it into focus so your experience is not simply a reality of restriction and constraint, a reality of non-events happening that you see within yourself are possible.

Many of you have beliefs that you hold to be truth. But when you look at these truths, you will begin to discover they have gaps in them, these truths of your being. Gaps that cannot be understood only from a physical reality and that need you to go beyond physical reality to a place of acceptance. There are indeed experiences that you cannot easily explain only by the rules and laws of the physical realm, and your physical situation.

This Awareness has spoken many times, that you had purpose when you came into this reality, that you chose to come into this physical life that you are now experiencing. In this there is also acceptance that you have chosen those challenges for yourselves that will indeed play out for you that will indeed confine and constrain you as long as you hold these to be your truths; such truths as the level of abundance, for example that you are experiencing in your life.

Many who hold the spiritual conception of themselves, hold that the material is corrupt and corrosive, and therefore, in the choices that are made, the lack of abundance is the reality many are experiencing. And with the lack of physical abundance there are those hardships that come along with this, such as not being able to have enough money to do the things you would love to do for yourself. Is this the truth of the situation or is this a belief?

Many are experiencing at this time great difficulty in accepting there are events happening on the planet at this time, that are very difficult and hard (not only for you yourselves as individuals) but for others, in particular the children of this planet at this time. Recently there have been events that have caused many of you great difficulty, emotional difficulty, mental difficulty, in accepting that the children are being treated the way they are. There has been in the country of the United States of America a situation that has arisen recently, where it has been brought to the attention of many, that children are being taken from their parents. These being the children of those who have come to the United States to find freedom to relieve themselves of the difficulties of their countries of origin, because of the situation that often exists in those countries they are coming from.

The mass media, the mainstream media, has most certainly been focused upon this in recent times and have presented the situation in such a way that it is highly emotional. It takes one's breath away to sense, or to know, that there are these problems for these poor children.

This Awareness would remind you that even these children who have been separated from their parents are also sovereign beings of spirit; have come here for their purpose as well as the purpose of the greater collective that is humanity. Part of that purpose is to bring to the attention of the world the situation that has been hidden for so long; this being the situation of abuse against children, of the use of children for nefarious reasons and purpose that lie in the realm of those who have had power and control for so long. In the presentation of the information of the situation, that which is your mainstream media, has chosen to present this information in ways that are indeed very emotive, very emotional, very grabbing at the very heartstrings of your being, to see children separated from their parents, put into detention.

This Awareness is not trying to justify this, or say it is all right, for it is not all right for the children to be treated this way. But what this Awareness would also point out, is as these are ones who are of Spirit themselves and as each has chosen to come into this life to have their experiences, to have their challenges, please understand these children also are here to help humanity itself awaken to that hidden truth that has been playing out for so long; the truth that there are those children who are trafficked, who are used and abused, who are murdered and sacrificed, for ones who would stay in power, ones who would feed off of them.

Presentation of the plight of these children, of these families, of these wonderful humans who have chosen to be here now as part of the unfolding reality that is dawning, are here from that level of spirit, that level of the supreme choice of spirit to partake in the events and circumstances of these times in order to elicit change. To spark that revolution of spiritual awakening that is underway.

Know that they are, too, part of a larger plan, a greater plan of Spirit Itself. And in their choice to present in this way, to be victims as alleged, as so, is alleged to be the case that this is also in co-operation with the purpose of Spirit Itself. It is not to ignore the plight of these children, but rather to awaken that this is no longer tolerable how the children are treated;

the plan of spirit being more than simply viewing the suffering of the children over your mainstream media. And through the presentation by ones in power, who wish to stay in power, of that which is emotional, which grabs one at the very pit of their being.

To understand also, that as they have chosen this, they are here not simply as victims but as warriors. Warriors who have come at this time to bring the light of spirit back into the darkness, to expose the situation as it really is, not only the actual situation of the detention of these children, but how children, how humans, are being used and abused and this has been so for some time. Remember also, the mainstream media is controlled, is used to perpetuate the situation. While it may seem these ones are victims, (these children, these families, are victims), if you understand that they as spirit beings have made choices and are part of the unfolding of events, it may help you come through that which *is* the situation of abuse on this planet, by seeing it exists and by being *intolerant* to the perpetuation of the situation any longer.

This you do at your own personal level. Some of you may wish to protest, may wish to write your congressman or woman, may wish to blog about it, speak about it, share this with others. But the most important thing to do and to remember is that as you are of spirit, and that as you are as creators in the reality of perception you are experiencing, to change your own attitude is what is of greatest importance. To understand that these wonderful ones who have come at this time, to be so present in the public attention, this is that which you support as the goal and purpose of shifting consciousness on this matter. Of no longer being tolerant to the hidden abuse and destruction of the children, and of those humans that do not quite understand the situation.

You are enlightened beings and as enlightened beings you are bringing *light* into the situation and it does start for each and every one of you in the core of your own being, in the perceptions of your own reality. Do not hold that it is okay for those who are the victims to be treated this way. Do remember that as spiritual beings these ones have chosen, just as you have chosen, to be here now, and to be part of the unfolding of spirit, the entering into the consciousness of humanity, which is the force of the Divine Source itself. As expressions of the Divine Source you have it within you to create the reality, that is your reality, no longer simply based on unconscious unknown principles or beliefs that are standing within you.

Bursting through these standing beliefs, breaking them down, realizing you have the option to shift and change the circumstances of *your* life, of *your* experience. In holding the truth of this, in participating in this awakening, you will find your own lives are mirrors of reflection to the situation of belief that you hold. And if that situation of belief holds that you are a victim to life, and you have no power to shift or change your circumstances, then this will be so, so powerful are you.

But if you hold that you can shift the conceptualization of reality you hold, and hold that as spirit beings, ones of greater magnitude than that which is prescribed, which is given to you as the state of being, then you will find the magic and the miracles of spirit reflecting in your life, each and every day. To hold this means you must be willing to re-evaluate many of the beliefs you hold as concrete, ironclad, and unbreakable. If this were so then there would be no point for this Awareness to be speaking to you at this moment.

But it is not so, and as you begin to alter the conceptions of reality that you hold, (that which you have been programmed into), you will find, step-by-step, shifts happening in the experience of your reality, and that which you have been confined and constrained by, that these principles drop away as those which are the new principles enter into the life, your life. And as this happens you will find miracles and magic in your life. As you align yourself to the inner and the hidden core of your being, and you no longer hold that you are restricted and constrained, and victims to the realities that have been forced upon you, but which you chose to experience in the first place. The presentation of your life will shift for you, will change for you.

Many of you reinforce constantly, negative beliefs, without ever understanding or recognizing you are doing so. Therefore what this Awareness is about to suggest might help shift you from those negative beliefs, those dark beliefs that are unconscious, that will bring them to the surface and on the surface, you can choose whether you wish to continue with these negative beliefs or not.

This Awareness presents a concept that some of you are certainly familiar with. And this is the concept of when one is using words that are considered swearing or bad words, there is a jar that you would put money in. Now, this is quite practical to reinforce the negative but is not as practical to reinforce the positive. In this concept, if one says a four-letter word, for example, and another says you have sworn, the expectation is that one puts money in the jar each and every time one swears, a swear jar. But as this Awareness has said, this is a negative perception and reinforces swearing.

However what if one were to take this very same principle and create not a negative container but a positive container, a positive jar. What if upon thinking a positive thought, one rewards oneself by putting a quarter in the jar for each positive thought that one would have?

As one begins to focus on the positive, it is the positive that expresses itself in life, in your personal life. Further to this, it could be the case indeed that when one has a negative thought, one becomes cognitive of that negative thought and shifts that negative thought from a negative expression of reality to a positive one. For example, a negative thought would be “there is not enough money in my life”, “my life is complicated and made much more difficult because of a lack of money, of scarcity", for it is a scarcity mentality that is the strongest conception of most, *not* the concept or an understanding of abundance.

Therefore, if one has a negative thought and one captures this negative thought instead of rewarding it, or reinforcing it, one shifts that negative thought. And instead of thinking you are a victim, you put forward the positive thought that,

"I am in control of my life".

"I am a creator being aligned with spirit".

"I am abundance and abundance flows to me".

When you have shifted from that negative stance to the positive stance, reward yourself. Put a quarter in the jar, or pat yourself on the back.

It is when you start to become more and more aware of the negative thoughts you hold, and the negative beliefs you hold, that is when you also have the possibility of changing them. And as you reward yourself for the *positive* thoughts you can and will change your life. And this is a given by Spirit for it is known by spirit that it is so. And as you are of spirit, you can make it so.

Therefore, this Awareness presents this is as a challenge to each and every one of you. To become more aware of those unconscious negative thoughts and beliefs. And when you become aware to shift them. To deliberately state a more positive belief that countermands the negative instruction, the negative belief system, and that introduces to each and every one of you a positive reality of your own experience.

This is the challenge this Awareness is presenting to you at this time. And as you discover, and as you experience a shift in your own personal reality, you expand this to include those ones who are at this time presenting themselves for humanity to see, and to understand, that it is no longer tolerable to use such ones or to allow in your personal experience, of your personal reality, such a reality to be part of your personal reality. You begin to hold that humanity itself is awakening and is stepping together, coming together, to change that which has been the stance of those in power for so long (that you are their victims, you are their sacrifices) and that they will continue to do so.

This is no longer the truth of the situation, for you will not hold it to be your personal truth, you will not hold it to be that which you wish to energize and to reinforce. Indeed it is the opposite now, that for each and every child that comes to your attention, you give thanks to their Divine Spirit, and to the greater spirit of Divine Source that has entered into the playing field at this time. And that this reality is no longer acceptable, and the positive reality of enlightened human beings who will not accept any longer this state of affairs that has been forced upon them for so long. This is no longer the case, it is done and dusted, and you are seeing this shift happening each and every day, both in your own personal reality and the experience you are having in the present moment, and also that which is the experience of humanity itself, both in your nation as well as globally.

These are the most exciting of times. These are the most magical and positive of times, and it is now for you to realize this, to be so *in your own lives*, in your own individual experience, of life itself. Life is that which happens while you are making other plans. Shift your plans away from the continuance of the restrictive state of consciousness to that which is the expansive, expansive and positive state of consciousness. Know that you are truly Creator Beings. Know and remember you are truly of Spirit, and the spirit you are here is the Warrior of Spirit, to bring change both into your own individual lives but also into the collective that is humanity at this time.

A Third Point of Reference

You are being asked to move to a third point of reference, a trinary point of referral

There have been ones who have stepped forward and presented themselves in a way that has caused this Awareness to challenge them, to ask them to look at a part of their own being that is unconscious and unseen to them. And this Awareness gives thanks to those who have played the role, to present it in such a way, allowing this Awareness to use them as examples.

You are all examples to yourselves and to others, but the journey itself is of a nature now that it does require much more commitment, much more intention, much more desire to break free of the restrictions and binds that have held you for so long. These are not ropes that have been put around your wrists, or shackles around your ankles that physically restrain you. They are of a mental nature; they are of an emotional nature.

And it is of greatest importance now for each of you to realize it is not the gross and obvious that you need to be looking for, but the subtle and the demure, the hidden that confines you and constrains you. And it is important for you to start to question, when you sense those moments of negativity. Why this is so? And does it need to be so? And will you hold it so? Or will you shift it? Will you put the spin of positivity into it? Will you hold it a different way?

You are welcome to make mistakes. Indeed this is the best way to learn. But where this Awareness speaks out against the mistakes, is only in holding and perpetuating them deliberately because you will not look at them. It has gone beyond the time of hesitancy and resistance, and yet it is the time of hesitancy and resistance.

Remember you live in a paradox, and you can hold both angles and both points. But you are also being asked to move beyond them to a third point of reference, a trinary point of referral. So you can see yourself not as a harsh complainer of self, not as a judge of self, but rather as one who lovingly embraces oneself and allows for the journey, even those bad hair days, even those moments of contempt against oneself. To flip it, to spin it out of the negative backing, to the light of the positive and of the Divine.

The journey continues. There are many events taking place, and indeed this Awareness would say to you today at this time, "Hold on to your hats", for much is about to break upon your shores in America, and upon the shores globally as well, that will shake things up.

And as they break, remember how important it is not to go into the fear, not to go into the negativity, but to spin it, to hold it, to be in the center of your circle, to stay in Divine sacred neutrality, and to watch as those matters unfold. And know that your intent and your desires are what will define your experience.

And that is why you hold it will all work out, it will finally come to pass, that which you have come here to be part of, which is the destiny of Humanity and of the planet Herself. It will be so, for it is held as so by Divine Source, and you are of Source. You are the Divine Source. And you hold it, and you hold it, and you hold it. And it will be so.

It is done. It is complete. It is so.

You Are Part of the Grand Design of Spirit

You are the sum total of much more than you have ever thought yourself to be

That which is Cosmic Awareness is now available and greets one and all, and says immediately to all that you are the sum total of much more than you have ever thought yourself to be. You are that focus point, that focus personality, that this Awareness has so often spoken of. And in this, there is the experience of complete attention to the fabric of one's life; the events, the circumstances, the individuals who are involved in that life so much so, it more often than not seems like there is nothing other than that which you are experiencing directly or indirectly.

But, what if it truly were so, that you are part of the fabric of Spirit Itself, part of the grand design of Divine Source and Spirit? What if as a small point of focus in your personal experiencing of this physical life, you are also giving to the collective a part of an experience that is so broad and so vast it is almost impossible to comprehend this from that perspective of the individual focus?

It becomes overwhelming to think of such matters for most. And so most do not choose to think of such matters, do not choose to open themselves up to the greater context of their own true life experience beyond the physical. And in this is that which has been the experiment of the ages, for the last thousands of years, to have such a unique and individual experience, that it is hard to remember who you truly are, or where you truly come from. Because this is so; because the connection to Spirit seems to be broken when you are in the physical body having the experience.

It is therefore difficult when one hears the words 'that you are more than what you think you are' to believe this, to know this to be so. And yet this Awareness says if you go beyond that which is the logic and the rational; that which is the mental quality of such thinking, you will find you often have a feeling for this. And this feeling does indeed support that premise that you are much more than you think you are.

This truly connects you to Source and it is a heart connection. For you are always connected to heart. And even though the nature of the experiment in consciousness was to come in to have your individual experience, and add it to the collective fiber of the Source Itself, that at the same time it is possible, with intent and purpose, to open yourself up to the greater expression of the Source as It speaks through you, as it speaks to you.

This may not be shared by many others, who are not there. But this is a time where that is the case still, that many still are separated from Spirit. Not truly separated, for there is always the connection to Spirit, but in terms of the experience that is being held to be so, that is experienced by most, it does mean that most are still at a point, and at a stage where they do not consider these grander issues. And are content to live within the framework of the assumed reality even when it comes to Source itself.

Most believe in a male entity being that is God, who somehow judges one and all. Now, this is of course a concept that while still held by the majority, is not the truth of the situation. But so it is that many have a concept of such an entity or supreme being where they are like children unto the Lord and in this trust of the Lord, the trust of God, there is that assumption that they will be taken care of, that all will be taken care of, and the responsibility of an individual is subjugated to this belief, is defined and shaped by this belief.

It is even so, that most politicians speak of such a faith. After all does the Queen not go to church on Sunday and does not Donald Trump express a belief in God above? But this does not mean necessarily that they believe this to be so. They believe it only in the sense that by expressing such a belief it is felt by those masses even, that it is so still, that God above is the one that controls all.

But you are coming out of this daydream, this false assertion of spirit and spirituality. For in the sense of giving over to another, one is not in control of their lives, ultimately. One is not part of a greater fabric of Spirit which is active and present all of the time.

This Awareness is not speaking out against such beliefs. These are the beliefs that are held by those who need to have such beliefs, for in the context of their present life experience, where they have chosen a path of experience, this is part of that path. And it is part of the process, and the journey of humanity itself, to go through the application of one's power and one's truth to another. Be it another in the form of a parent, be it another in the form of a teacher, or a priest, or a politician, or a sovereign ruler.

Now, is the time, to start to question this, to the point that it would seem to those who are the supporters of such beliefs heretic, heretical rather. But what is heresy but the expression of something other then what most believe in? And in this you are all heretics. Heretics in the sense that you have questioned, that you have looked at, and are looking at, the events and circumstances on the planet at this time. And, that includes all of the actors. And many of you have questioned indeed the assumptions of religions that assert a supreme being hold sway over all, and you must live the life in accordance to what is commanded by that being. And yet most of the history behind this is false, most of that which is held to be so, is inaccurate, and fake news.

Does this mean you can deal with others with disrespect for they hold such beliefs? You cannot! You must always have respect for those who have beliefs other than yours. And it is not, rather at this *time*, it is not yet the matter of squashing the beliefs of others.

It is the time still of *recognizing* the beliefs of others, and your *own* beliefs. And rather than force your beliefs on to others or even to engage in argument with others, it is more than the time to simply let it be for others. But to take full and complete responsibility for yourselves, and your own beliefs, and your own programming.

Many do not even recognize how deep the programming runs. And how total it is. For this, one simply has to look at where one goes into fear, when one has a thought of doing things differently. For example, many hold scarcity as the model of existence, there will never be enough and you are taught this is so.

You are programmed to believe this is so, therefore you must acquire money somehow. For the majority, acquiring money means working hard, saving, being diligent, making financial sacrifices so that one has enough money to exist.

Then in this there is the element of fear that is added, when one senses they are not wealthy enough, they do not have enough, they do not have enough for the pension and retirement and how will they exist, how will they live, how will you live? But this is the programming of humanity that you have acquired, because it was the choice to have such an experience. The truth of the matter is that you are abundance. And as you hold yourself open to receive abundance it will come to you. As you hold yourself open to receive miracles, they will come to you. Because this is the truth of the matter, despite the programming.

Last session, last teleconference session, this Awareness spoke of the thought of creating a 'positivity pot' or what this Awareness would also call a 'posi-pot'. The point of this posi-pot, this pot of positivity, is to help you start to see through the programs you are running unconsciously. To help you realize how often it is the program has you, especially when you go into fear, when you have that overwhelming fear that things will not go well, or you do not have enough money, or you are not loved or accepted.

Every time you have this type of action or reaction to the circumstances of your life, take a moment. Shift away from that negative view, that negative belief, that negative program. Remind yourself that you are not about scarcity or that it is a denial of abundance, but rather you are abundance. Abundance flows to you not only in terms of wealth and money but in all matters. As you do this, you reward yourself. You can quite literally reward yourself by throwing a buck or two into your posi-pot.

But the more important matter is seeing that you are coming from programming, seeing you are coming from a place of your beliefs. And if they are negative in nature, and it is unconscious how they rule you, breaking this unconscious rule is what is of greatest importance. And that is why the suggestion of the positivity pot, a posi-pot, is made to you all. How you reward yourself is your business. But it is imperative now, especially now, to break away and out of the programming that each and every one of you chose to experience upon coming into this life, even the programming of a false deity that calls itself God.

There is indeed the God force, the Godhead, the energies of the Divine Source that is always there. And you do not have to be born in a state of original sin. You do not have to be the criminal against the divine supreme Lord male above, to experience that which is your true Source. And Source is within you and you are part of Source.

Right now, you are all in the situation of seeing through the false scenarios, the fake news, that is occurring on your planet at this time. And because this is so, you will present yourself with the challenges to your lives at this time, to help you break free, to come out of the programming; to recognize each and every one by nature of being on the planet having this physical life experience, has chosen the programming.

This is a good thing if you wish it to be. It is a bad thing if you wish it to be. It is your choice. And rather than to beat up on yourself thinking why have I made such bad choices or why is it so that I cannot free myself, simply shift it, go to a positive, go to an expression of a new belief. Indeed you are abundance and abundance flows to you. You are indeed here to be part of the solution and not part of the problem.

It was one year ago, at the time of the eclipse in the United States of America, this Awareness first mentioned the image of a zipper being unzipped across the length and breadth of the United States of America. Since that time, much of the goo and ooze and the putridness and poison and toxicity that has lain under the surface for so long, started to come out.

A year has passed and this Awareness asks you to look at the world at this time. Much is starting to come out. Of course, it is in the United States of America that the main play is being played. But this does not mean this is not occurring around the world. And it certainly does not mean that in countries that are not America, there are not also challenges of leadership, and beliefs, and programming, and power establishments that are taking place. All of this is global indeed. But, in America where the eclipse occurred, that which has been the hidden poison has been coming to the surface.

This Awareness has also spoken that the years 2017, 2018, 2019 to 2020 are critical years; this three-year period in particular, 2017 to 2020. And you are halfway through this period of time. And there is more coming. Indeed, this Awareness says it is just now that the push back of the Divine Source is being felt is starting to come to the surface itself. But do not be overwhelmed by the poisonous nature of that energy, of those who have had power and control for so long, who have always kept it hidden. Do not be upset that it is now much more visible. You are in a war, make no mistakes about it.

It is not your traditional and classic war where bombs are dropped and bullets launched; it is rather a war of technology, it is a war of the psyche, of psychological proportions, but it is a war fully engaged. And, rather than be negative or come from that fear place on this matter, hold the positive that it is being released so it can be cleansed and cleared and that Divine Source is behind it all and there is indeed a big plan. Trust the plan. But that plan is much more than the workings of humans, it is the plan of Divine Source itself. And you are also, each of you, part of the plan.

And as those events unleash that are now kicked back to the control and power that has been held hidden for so long, as that which was hidden is brought to the surface and exposed so it may be cleaned up, so it may be cleansed, know you too are part of the solution, part of the workings of Divine Source. For each of you are of Divine Source, you are each and every one a pinpoint in Divine consciousness having your experiences. And those experiences include the unconscious programming that you are coming through. And, it includes the leaders that are now present who are working to drain the swamp, to clean things up. And as you hold it to be so, both in your personal life and in the life of your nations and in the life of the planet itself, it will become so.

Before the beginning today of this session with Awareness, Will and Callista heard a song many of you are familiar with. It is the song 'A Never-Ending Story' and this was sent to them as a proof that Spirit is available. It is that which you could call an act of synchronicity but it was more than that. It was sent to remind them that with the dream, if you have the dream, and believe the dream, it will be, and that the story is indeed never ending. There will be other stories ahead just as there are other stories behind. The past proves the future.

But this Awareness would say for each of you is that you are in the moment, and the moment is now. And as you open up to the deeper nature of your being, and as you defeat your own programs and lift yourself high, you will find that the communication with your own being, with your high self, and thus with Source as well, will present itself in ways that will astound you, that will uplift you, that will be the miracles you have been seeking all of your life. The communication will be direct. It will come to you in the very moments of the greatest need, where the challenges are the greatest of all. To go beyond that which you have always known to be so. To be open to the magic and the miracles of the Divine Source and to remember you are that, you are the magic, you are the miracles, you are Source itself.

It is now time to remember yourselves. To remember the truth of who and what you really are, and no longer to accept the lies and the propaganda and the conditioning and the programming of ones who have kept you slaves for so long. In the eyes of the Divine Source you are not slaves at all but extensions of itself, into an experience of consciousness. As you remember this, and as you remember yourself, you will find the miraculous is your norm, your new norm. And that the communications with the Divine Source are direct and through the heart and are always available to you. And there will be those incidents of synchronicity that will confirm this to you, that will support you, always. For it always has been so that you have been supported and are supported and will always be supported by the Source itself.

You are far greater than anything you have ever been told yourself or told to yourself or told by others to you than you are. You are the Divine Source itself, having the unique experience that is you.

Be Prepared

There is indeed that which will be of the greatest significance in the shifting of consciousness that is ready to occur at this time —

That which is Cosmic Awareness is available and is here today to speak out, and to say to one and all that these are urgent times. And this Awareness has now a message, even that which you could call a warning to these urgent times. That is felt there is indeed that which will be of the greatest significance in the shifting of consciousness that is ready to occur at this time. In fact this Awareness would even say it is already underway. In accordance to that which is the energies on the planet at this time, but especially the energies in America, this is a time to be prepared.

That the one who is known as Donald Trump most recently gave out a warning to be prepared, to be ready for any and all events. Now it is interpreted by many that this is in regards to physical preparedness, and this is correct to some degree. This Awareness does say that it is wise to have supplies available in excess to what you might normally have, or at least feel comfortable that which you have already accumulated in terms of supply will be sufficient to having a period of time where there may be disruptions to the availability of supplies on all levels.

But this Awareness also says it is a time to be mentally and psychologically and spiritually prepared. While it is all right of course to be physically ready, one must also be psychologically ready for events that could prove to be the turning point in that which has been a war, a war on the deep state, a war on those who have had power and control for so long that they assume it is their right always to have such power and such control over the populace, be it the populace of a nation or even globally.

That therefore there is a type of arrogance that is still held by the deep state that gives them the sense and the feeling they will be successful in their adversity, that they will successfully control the minds of the masses to such a degree that the masses will just believe those lies and those deceptions being run on the populace, in this case primarily the populace of the United States of America. But again this Awareness says this is a global event that is going down.

This Awareness has often spoken of the need to be diligent, and to have one's B*S* meter running. It is especially important at this time, when those lies that are being put out are not simply little lies, but are actually big whoppers, whoppers of lies of such an intense energy that many can feel it very, very strongly.

Now, this Awareness has always said to question everything, to question all. That means when reports come out that seem to indicate for example that Donald Trump is isolated in the White House, and there is a resistance movement of his own people against him, this is believed to be so because some anonymous source wrote some anonymous piece for the New York Times. Why should you believe this?

This Awareness says, do not believe the lies that are coming, and they will come very fast and furious. It is of the most incredible importance now, in the preparations you are mentally undertaking, to ask the questions, to not just believe the mass media, even though they come across so convincingly.

How many for example have actually questioned whether this article that was written for the New York Times is in itself the truth, that someone from Donald Trump's staff really wrote this?

It was not written by any from the Trump team, but the allegation that it was, and then the pushing of this lie over the mass media certainly has many wondering about whether it could be so. But this is how they deceive. This is how they hook you into a belief that because it has been spoken and it is being put out there so vehemently by the deep state, that there must be something to it.

This Awareness says there is nothing to it other than that which you believe. And if you choose to believe the lies without asking your questions, without going to your B*S* meter and feeling that which is the energy behind the lie, then certainly these ones could be successful in diverting attention away from what is really happening.

That which is really happening is an action so deep and intense by Trump and his crew, including the "Q" team, that they are on the very edge of exposing the liars and the deceivers. They are on the very edge of taking the actions that have been underway for some time.

Many are frustrated. Those who know that this has been a war of a great significance, and that this war is about the very future of humanity itself, those who have had this knowing and sensing have become very frustrated. Because it still seems like even though much information is being put out, no action seems to be happening.

This too is part of the deception of the deep state, to give the impression it is actually the opposite, the action is going against Trump, and his own people are turning against him.

Again, this is the lie. And each of you have the capacity to sense this out, and to feel this out, and not to be swept up by it, not to be taken deep into the fabric of the lie.

But it does take responsibility for each and every one to say, not on my watch, I will not support this lie and this deception. And if even though many do believe it, I will hold that it is the exact opposite. How many times has this Awareness said that you are creator beings? And it is imperative now that you fully appreciate and understand that, but even more that you live this.

Recently this Awareness spoke of the importance of creating a positivity pot, or a posi-pot. This is more an attitude of positivity than an actual pot that you can throw a quarter in, or a dollar in when you are positive. The importance is because, as creator beings, if you do not realize how effective you are as creator beings, and you still go with the old programming the Low Self has taken on board, which could also be called the mind control and brainwashing of deep state, of humanity itself, then it is so that your reality will reflect that which is of a negative order, that which puts out the fear that perhaps it will all go sideways, it will all go South, that these ones are stronger then, or perhaps what they are saying is the truth of it, which it is not.

As a creator being you largely create from the place of the Unconscious. It is why this Awareness has spoken so often of the need to find that truth within, but more importantly even, to do the work that needs to be done so you are connected to your Low Self, that which is the interface of third dimensionality, that which creates the third dimensional reality you are experiencing, as well as connecting.

And many seem to forget this over and over, that if they do not do the work, and if they do not find the multi-dimensionality of their own being in their focus personality, where the Low Self, the Middle Self, and the High Self are one with each other, where there is open and deep communication with the Low Self and the High Self, and that the Middle Self begins to awaken to the truth of its own being. If this does not occur, then it is so easy to shepherd you along, down that narrow track way to the pens that will hold you, that lie just over the rise of the hill.

These are the most critical of times. And you must be prepared now to hold as you have never held before, the positive attitude and belief that this is the turning point from that which is Paradox. It has been the turning point for quite some time now. But you are getting to that cutting edge again, where the importance of holding to that which is known within you as the reality that supersedes the physical third dimensional reality most are conditioned to believe in, that by holding this to be so and not deviating, not releasing your strength in that department, in belief it will work out because it is meant to work out, it has the very deepest endorsement of Spirit, Divine Source itself.

For it has been so, and is so, that the future is the result of the past, and that in the future, humanity will travel a completely different path. But if it is so in the future, then it is also so now, this being the turning point, this being the point of no return. This Awareness has also spoken many times of tracks, timelines of consciousness that can be followed.

This Awareness can say to you there are time tracks, timelines that will lead to the Planet B scenarios, where those who are the ones who have been the dictators and the despots and the tyrants, those who have had the power for so long, will continue to hold power. But you do not have to follow those time tracks. You do not have to participate or be part of them. It is your choice.

And as a creator being with full capacity to create that which you can experience as the truth of your life, as you take more control of your life and of your function as a creator being, then the time track you will follow will not be the Planet B scenario. It will be the new balance of Planet AB, the new dualistic reality that is about to emerge.

Even beyond this however, lies the energy of the fifth dimension and that which this Awareness has called the

Planet A scenario. This scenario is of a nature, that as you open up to your multi-dimensional being, you bring it into focus and thus the experience the effect of those energies of consciousness that come from that which is fifth dimensional, where you can certainly redefine and recreate the reality that is your experience. This is the place of magic and wonder, joy, and love. This is the place where you see your life opening up, and you are guided easily with grace into the future, the future that is held to be so, the future that is of the High Spirit and the high energies you have access to.

Simply because it does not seem to happen in your life, does not mean that which this Awareness is speaking of cannot happen. Indeed it is actually an indicator that you have more work to do, this being the work of redefining yourself, of finding that connection with the Low Self and the High Self, and merging all three together in the oneness of self. And in this oneness of self, all things are possible.

When you hesitate, when you deny, when you fall victim to what others say, or feel you must live your life in accordance to the expectations of others who hold the lesser reality to be so, then you are giving up your authority as a creator being. This does not mean you are not creating. It simply means you are still unconscious to the actual strength and power you have to create the reality that is in alignment and accordance to your own high spiritual nature.

Many of you have had now experiences of ease and grace in your lives. What this means is, that when you are in alignment to the high spiritual source, and your own soul memory, life presents opportunities that flow into your life. It is not the struggle that many hold it to be. It is not just a journey of suffering, but rather a joyous experience of how it can be when you are in that alignment, when you are tuned in to the energies of your own high spiritual being and high spiritual self. This is where the wonder occurs, and this is where the magic and miracles happen. And it can become part of your everyday reality.

And as the adventure unfolds, what you begin to experience more and more is not the struggle of life that you are told it is, not the suffering and the pain, not the sense of abandonment, but a genuine and continuous revelation of your own spiritual being, of that which is the truth of who you truly are, beyond the contacts and confinement of reality shaped by others, be it ones in your family, be it amongst your peers and associates, be it regionally or nationally or even globally.

These dark ones, these ones of the elite, the cabal, the deep state, have always known this and have always manipulated so those who are their slaves, their subjects, their prey, do not wake up to this truth. And in doing so they have always thus had the privilege of being the elites, of being those who have the advantage. This advantage is now gone.

And these ones are now very desperate in their actions. And therefore they will commit atrocities, even, to ensure humanity does not wake up. It is not required that humanity wakes up. What is required is that each of you, as an individual focus personality, wakes up.

And as you awaken to the truth far beyond anything you have ever been told before, ever been led to believe before, your life will change. It is already changing. Even in the month that has just occurred, there have been tremendous steps forward that are largely unseen by the general public, because they have not seen deeper than that which is in front of their noses, and that which they are told to believe in.

For those of you who are hearing the voice of this Awareness, this Awareness reminds you that it is you, and you alone, that define and create your reality. And if you are doing so from the place of unconscious beliefs that are negative in nature, if you energize these beliefs and hold them to be the truth, then it will be so. But you are not that. And you have the creative power to be positive, to affirm that you are part of the solution, and not part of the problem.

Therefore at this time, this Awareness sends you all its energies to help you awaken, to help you find that level of trust and belief, that which you are attracted to, that which appeals to you, that which is your spiritual truth, is indeed the truth by which you live your life. You have nothing to lose. But you have everything to gain if you hold this as the way of your life.

Hold On To Your Own Reality

Pull yourself through into that which is the expression of the Divine itself —

That this brings this Awareness truly to the end of today's session, today's gathering. The month before, since the last gathering, has been a very powerful and active month. And it is seen the month ahead will be equally so, if not even more intense.

And this Awareness asks you to remember, as those things unfold around you, not to be drawn into the falseness of the intent of others who would continue to dominate and control. But rather to hold that you as that intense focus personality of Spirit, Divine Source itself, are calling in the new reality, and the new order of your own being, and the new experience that is unfolding for all of humanity.

And it will be so, that while there are many who have vested interest in outcomes, you do not need to have such a vested interest, in that you already hold what it will be and what will be so. For it has already been played out, and all that remains is to fill in the details. And as you hold it to be so, it will be so. For it is your intent, not only as the one you are, but also the intent of the one that you express through you, the one that is the Divine Source, the eminence of the Everything and the All.

And in this place of your Divine Nature you have that which is the responsibility of your point of focus, that which is the intent and desire you have as the individual you are in this present reality. This can be the most exciting and rewarding of times or it can be the most hellish of times. It is your right to choose.

But as this Awareness sees that you have come here to be part of the solution, you can pull yourself forward, pull yourself through into the expression of the Divine itself, knowing itself in this place of limitation and restriction. And as you understand this in yourself, and as you understand the nature of your own spiritual source, and that which you are, you will not be able to fully see life as it once was, because it is completely understood by you that things are simply not what they seem to be, unless you wish it to be so. Know this in the month ahead.

Know you are prepared, because on that level of Source and Spirit, of Knowingness, you are prepared. And that there will be the flexibility needed by you, to simply shoot the rapids, to go on a wondrous adventure, to know that no matter what unfolds, you are already in alignment to what will be, which is the intent of the Source itself, Divine Source itself.

And as you commit yourself to the experiencing of this, the unfolding of the Divine Source's will, you will see that your life will indeed become the life of ease and grace that this Awareness speaks to you of, because it is in alignment with Divine Source, your own source, that you will find the miracles and magic that await you. For this is as it is, and so shall it be.

This Awareness honors each and every one of you, each and every unique expression of the Divine Source, and says to you that this Awareness is part of you, as well as you are part of this Awareness. Remember this always, for this Awareness walks with you in all ways and always. And it is so.

Storms in September

There is at this time a War that is raging, a War of great significance —

This Awareness says these are indeed interesting times, and one can look at this as either the ancient Chinese curse of living in interesting times or the acceptance there are energies about now, that have made it so. These are interesting times because there are the energies of the Divine Source itself that are very much interceding into the events and affairs of humanity at this time. For most this is not something that is noticeable, and many are coming from that perspective of only the events they are observing. To this end this Awareness says that these interesting times deserve much scrutiny and consideration and each individual must ask themselves why are the events happening that are unfolding, especially those events in the United States of America.

There is at this time a war that is raging. It is not a war of bombs and bullets necessarily. But it is nonetheless a war of great significance between those who would maintain their power and privileges, those who would maintain control over the populace versus those who would break this control and this power; those who are setting up the evidence that exposes these ones as being deceivers, as being those who have a hidden agenda. Many call those of the shadow realm 'Deep State', while those who oppose them are the ones that are trying to bring light into the darkness and truth into consciousness.

The truth that these ones who have had privilege and control and power for so long, are not there to benefit either the people of the United States of America nor humanity itself. The one who is leading the opposition against those who are the elites, those who are the cabal, those who are Deep State, is the one known as Donald Trump. And he is a man that is very intriguing to say the least. This war that is raging would paint him as not only a fool and an ignorant despot, but also as one who cannot be trusted; one who is a danger to the people of America themselves. But who is it that are leveling these charges? Who is it that is leading the attack on Trump and those he represents and leads?

It is those who have had the privilege for so long, who are being exposed, they know they are being exposed, and who are doing anything and everything they can, to mislead and misalign the American people to the truth of the situation. Their situation is desperate and they know this. They speak of fear as that which Donald Trump uses to get his own way; fear to the populace that there are dangers there that only he can remedy and deal with. This is a type of projection away from those who are actually responsible for these crimes against the people of America and against humanity, and level it towards Donald Trump, and Qanon, and those who are here now actively promoting the truth, the truth of the situation that has so long reigned upon this planet, and in America.

It is up to each and every individual to be of open mind. To be in balance. To be available to detect and discern the truth when it presents itself. Those who have had dominion and charge for so long, have also the control of the mainstream media. The press, the channels and the reports that are given against Trump are from the mainstream media, who have as an agenda to spin the truth, to project that which they themselves are covering up against the one, and those who would expose the truth: This being Trump and his crew.

Now it is easy to be fooled and misled. And that is why this Awareness recommends that one have this openness and balance, this discernment, that one uses that which this Awareness has often called the BS meter, to sense out the truth, feel out the truth. These are very interesting times indeed, but they are also critical times, especially in this month of September. There is indeed a war raging, and one can also understand that the storms are coming quite literally so, in America and around the world. But also the storm will be unleashed as evidence is unleashed; as evidence is released to the public.

Bear in mind that you and you alone, each of you as individuals, have the right to discern the truth, if you are willing, and if you are able. This means there is a responsibility upon the shoulders of each individual to look at this truth, to feel it out, to seek more information, to validate those claims from both sides and to see what works for you, what feels right for you.

This is no longer a time where one can dig the hole and hide themselves in that hole, avoiding the events that are being unleashed at this time, and the truth that goes with it. In these critical times, often it is not direct action that is required, it is direct perception of the truth which will set one free. And then to have the courage to hold that, to speak it, to share it, if and when appropriate. Now is the time to realize that which was unleashed already over a year ago with the eclipse in the United States, has come truly to the surface. And that quagmire of toxicity which lay below the surface has indeed been released. And this too is part of the energies that all are experiencing at this time.

Stand vigilant. Stand strong. Hold the truth in your heart, and know the truth will indeed set you free. And these are the times that have been predicted as being the end times. This does not mean an end to America, or an end to humanity. It simply means that which was the norm for so long is no longer the norm, and extraordinary events are taking place right now. Even if the mainstream media is covering up, is spin doctoring the truth, is leading that assault upon Trump personally to demote him, to misalign him, to confuse the many.

It is underway, and these interesting times do require that sense of purpose and commitment to the truth, and the release of the truth. And this is exactly what is happening, and each individual must determine for themselves their own personal truth.

Be vigilant. Be strong. Be the ones who are the heralds of the truth that shall set you free personally, and shall set the country free as well.

Politics and the Great Spiritual Awakening

The political atmosphere that is current is actually part of a spiritual movement —

That which is Cosmic Awareness is now available and greets one and all in indeed these historical times. Often when you are involved in historical times, you do not even realize that it is so. And yet, if you look back on your own lives, your personal lives, and look at the many events that have happened to you, and to the planet, to humanity, over the last decades you will see there have been many events you could indeed consider to be historical events.

But this Awareness must say, that at this time in particular, the energies are higher than they have ever been. For huge changes are taking place, shifts in consciousness are underway. It is so that it seems to be focused on one man, this man being the president of the United States Donald Trump. But this would be erroneous, in that he is part of a bigger plan, he is part of a bigger working of the events and circumstances on the planet. He is a focus point most definitely, and through him and that which this Awareness would call his team, this being not only Q and the Qanon, but all who are at this time working towards bringing change, first to the nation of the United States of America, but also globally as well.

Many think it is indeed only a situation that is occurring in the United States with a man who has a huge ego, who seems very self-centered and absorbed. They do not see that the team he has constructed around him is very much part of the underlying change that is taking place. Also, this is not simply about the United States of America although it is the focus point; but rather a global event, that is very much challenging the Deep State around the planet. And the Deep State both in the United States, and all other countries, are very panicky at this time, for what is underway, what is going on.

The curiosity is, while most see it only as events unfolding in the United States, very few either understand it is a global event and as well a very personal event. That is why, even though there seems to be a preoccupation with politics, that the political atmosphere that is current is actually part of a spiritual movement. For indeed if the planet, the various governments and countries, cannot shift away from that which has been the oppressing influence and control of what you could call Deep State, the Cabal, the New World Order, the Elites - the names go on and on - if this cannot and does not happen, then that track that will be taken will be one with dire consequences.

Now having said this, this Awareness would still assert that it is all still up to the individual. For even though the success of deep state would mark the negative, if you step out of the negative yourselves, if in your own life you look at your life as the one who is the focus of that life and while you can see the external events that are happening for these are external events, but realize that what is of even greater importance is the internal events of your own life, your own personal focus, what you are creating, what you are doing in your life, how you hold your energies, how you hold your focus. These are of the greatest importance.

As this Awareness just said, the external events are very important and one looks at them. But to think that if on the external plane of things those changes that happen will be what determines your life, then you still have not gotten it. You've still not gotten the point of you being the creator being, of you being the real focus. For all of life is through your own sensors, your own observations, your own interpretations of life itself. Of your life itself.

As this Awareness has said so many times in the past, when you look only to the external and expect your life will change because some external events change, and that this is what will change your life, then you have not realized the real importance of your own being, of your own greater being, of your own multi-dimensional being, as this is the most important matter of all. This Awareness would say then, that it is still of incredible importance to find your internal dialogue, your internal focus, your internal connections to that which is source, to that which is spirit, to that which is your own being as a sovereign spiritual being, contained within the context of an experience that is a collective experience, that is a global experience, that is a personal experience.

If you use the personal experience as your starting point, it is amazing how, once this is more in alignment with Source, the events in your life will adjust themselves to be of service to you, just as you are being of service to Source. You will also realize the external events start to shift and change, so you are not a victim to those external events, but rather the master of your own life, your own reality, your own universal consciousness and participation in that which is the greater picture.

Does this work? This Awareness assures you that it works, but the assurance of this Awareness is meaningless if you do not feel it yourself, understand it yourself, believe it yourself. As you put yourself into the influence of others, be it at the family level, be it at a municipal or local level, be it at a national level or even the global level, if you do not realize that you are the first contact, that you are the first contact with that which is of a greater essential essence than you are but you are part of it.

Therefore this paradox is that you are part of the greater existence of Source itself, and Source is expressing itself through you, so that you can have the unique individual experience of a sovereign being, that is here participating on many levels. And in those many levels there are opportunities always to return back to that original focus, that original understanding of your uniqueness and your importance as a spiritual sovereign being that is having a personal experience in the physical realm.

That this is a process this Awareness has often spoken this. It is a process, it is not simply that because this Awareness says it you are subject to it, and understand it, and make it so immediately. This process does involve much inner work, and that inner work is that which this Awareness has spoken to you many times, this process of understanding yourself as first and foremost a multi-dimensional being, in this multi-dimensional universe.

As you begin to connect with those two parts of your being, which is the high self and the low self, and you put yourself in the midst as the middle self, you unify your being. This puts you in greater alignment to the essence of the divine itself, the essence of spirit itself, focusing itself through you into the perception of reality, your reality, the reality of mother Earth, and the collective on her, on the planet itself. All of this is unique and special, but meaningless if you do not understand this point, if you do not make it so for yourself.

The irony perhaps, is that it does not matter if you do it or not. For you as a sovereign being have every right to make choices other than that which returns you back to that alignment and attunement to your own Source being. As such, that which is your opportunity is always available, whether in this life or another. Understand as well, that after the completion of this life, you do a review of your life. And you will realize what the original intent and purpose of the soul was, and whether or not you completed this, or even came close to the mark.

There is no judgment, whether you did it right or wrong, good or bad. The soul itself and you as the focus personality, will simply review what you have seen in that life, what you experienced in that life, whether you got it right in that life for your growth and development. And if you find in that review you did not get it quite right, then all this offers is another opportunity for the soul to project later again another focus personality. But in the meanwhile, while you are here having this experience, you have tremendous opportunity to make great strides in your own spiritual development and the evolvement of the soul itself. That is why it is of critical importance in this lifetime, to do as much as you can, to assure yourselves that you have made every effort. So when you return upon reviewing your life, you will see that you did it as well as you could. And this is of greater importance.

Another factor that is of great importance, when you return back to spirit, is a fundamental question that is presented to each soul, each focus personality as it returns back to the soul source. This is the question, "How many did I serve", a secondary question involved is "How many did I serve and how well did I serve them, how well did I serve". Again, there is no judgment here. But as you entertain this question in your lives, as you look at it as you move along, you will realize that service is part of the life journey. But the greatest service first and foremost is to Source, is to Spirit itself, and as you are of Spirit, as you are Spirit, then that question also includes your own reflection on how you are doing in this lifetime. Are you serving yourself first and foremost?

As one realizes this too is part of the question, and in the service of self, when you have those opportunities to work towards greater spiritual awareness and understanding, you will move into those opportunities with a different framework of reference,a different way of thinking about things. You will see that as you seek your own internal dialogue and connection, that this moves you, this changes you. As a result people see this, people understand this, and as they understand without understanding why they understand, they're coming from a deeper place of recognition. Then it is not a matter of you preaching to anyone about what is and what is not. It is simply about you living as this one who is of an exemplary personality, an exemplary expression of how it could be. These are all factors for your consideration.

There is a final area this Awareness would speak to today. And this is the area of that which could be called the mirrors of self reflection. There is much talk recently of that which is projection. Certainly it is heard in the observations of the different ones who are observing the political events that are underway. And there is much talk of how the Democrats are projecting their true nature upon their opponents, the Republicans, upon Trump, and there are many allegations of evil and personalities that are egocentric etc. But these are what are called projections, and often those cries against others are not really about others, but about themselves.

Now, if you take this concept of projection and shift it slightly, to look at it as not necessarily just projection upon others of that which you are guilty of yourself, but rather opportunities to look into your own mirror of reflection, self-reflection. If you see your life as one where when you speak of others in such a way that deflates them, or puts them down, or makes them guilty of whatever, this is a mirror of reflection that this Awareness would ask you to look at. For often as it is so that most hold the victim mentality, a victim will blame everything on others, will blame things on events and circumstances without ever looking at oneself. But if you can look into your mirror of reflection, look straight into your own eyes and be open to what you see, rather than shattering the mirror if it is not something you want to see, then this Awareness again assures you that this will move you, this will shift you, this will change you.

A willingness to look at those projections that one puts out there, a willingness to look into the mirror of reflection, is required of any who are spiritual in nature and who are seeking to evolve spiritually. This is therefore always a necessity for spiritual seekers. And when one has occasion sometimes to blame others, one may quickly realize upon looking into the mirror of self-reflection and reflecting on that image, reflecting on what is being projected, one will then have an opportunity to realize that the blame on others, the assumption of victimhood does not serve you, and does not move you forward. As a willing participant in this journey, who is willingly looking at him or herself in order to grow and expand, this is what is required of the spiritual seeker, as well as any understanding of the spiritual principles.

Many are involved at this time in what this Awareness could call tie-dye, butterflies, and rainbows. They want it all to be very nice, all very comfortable, all in accordance to what their thinking is in regards to Spirit and Spiritualism. This is part of the equation certainly to look positively on things, to hold that you have the capacity and power to shift and change things as you do. But if you are not willing to look at the darker side sometimes, and this being your own personal dark side, or those areas where there is not enough light coming in yet. This is that which will qualify you, which would restrict you, which would prevent you, from finding the true balance of your own being. And in that balance you will see that there is the light and there is the dark, and these two in balance create a wholeness just as the Yin/Yang symbol shows you, the white teardrop and the black teardrop, but it is all part of a whole. It is all part of the construct of Spirit itself, expressing itself in all ways, in the light and in the dark.

And as you look into that mirror of self-reflection, instead of loathing or fear, or confusion, one can open up and say

this too is me, and that I can do better, but I do not reject that which I see. It is there for me to see so it can guide me. So that I can grow and expand, and move into the wholeness of my own being, my true being, that being of a spiritual seeker, that being of a sovereign soul that is having this wonderful and unique experience. I am not qualified or defined by the outside events, I can observe them, I can stay neutral, I can grow with them, but they do not define me, they do not make it so. What makes it so is who I am within, what I am within. And as you discover this uniqueness of your own spiritual being, as you rise up in that spiritual awareness of the essence of who you are and what you are, that your life will shift, and change, and grow, for that is how it is.

There is Order in the Chaos

You are here to participate, but even more, you are here to assist this shift, this change in consciousness —

The Source is truly within you, and you are truly part of the Source, of the everything of the all, of that which is Divine Source and Spirit. You are unique, you are special, and you are ones who have chosen to be here now. You are in historic times, you are in the most amazing and exciting of times. You are not alone, you're not abandoned. There is order to the chaos. There is purpose behind the insanity. And that as you understand your own connections to your own deep and Divine Source you will find this connection, this knowing, this innerness, is that which will support you and carry you through these chaotic times.

Understand, as this Awareness has said to you, the frequencies have increased and are increasing daily. And that which is the intent, design and purpose of Source itself, to the shift in consciousness that is necessary at this time, is that which is being pursued by many. And you are here to participate, but even more you are here to assist this shift, this change in consciousness.

It does not mean you must go out and stand on a soapbox and preach the word to those who are standing there. It simply means you live this life with full understanding and awareness that you are more. You have always been more. And as you understand this in yourself, and you live it in accordance to the deep understanding of self, your life will reflect this.

And as your life reflects it, no matter what chaos is going on around you, you yourself will find the stability and balance needed. And others will see it and others will be attracted to it. As you give up the role and the mantle of victimhood, and as you take on board responsibility and effort to find the inner connection, this will lead you again to this place of balance, to this centeredness of being, to this connection to that which is beyond you, but within you as well.

And even though the planet may be in chaos, even though your nation may be in turmoil, it is all truly part of the bigger plan. It is all part of the Source and the Source's willingness to go through that which is needed to clear away confusion, darkness and miscomprehension.

And as you awaken to the truth of your own being more and more each and every day, you will find yourself moving forward each and every day. And even when challenge comes, it is all right to go into the darkness of challenge, as long as you seek the light within that will restore you, that will pull you back, that will bring the stability and the purpose of your life again to you.

These are indeed historical times. But you have chosen these historical times, you have been here before, you have been other places of other times, other historical times on other planets, in other galaxies. And this is one reason you have all come here now, because you are the experienced ones, you are ones who had knowledge and knowing of similar events.

But this is, of course, at the same time a unique event. Remember, that you are here because you have chosen to be here but you are here also because you are experienced. You may not remember this experience, this knowledge, but it is there within you. And again this is that which emphasizes the importance of making inner contact, finding the answers that lie within you.

This Awareness senses a readiness, and this readiness is individual, it does not say each of you must do it the same way, for each of you are unique and individual but each of you are part of Source, and part of Spirit. Remember this always. And as you seek the answers within, simply know they are there to be found. And if they do not come to you instantly have faith, have patience, have trust, and know that as you continue your inner search it will be found.

You will find yourself, and in the finding of yourself you will know and realize who you truly are, what you truly are.

This Awareness sends its light, its love, and its blessings to you always and in all ways.

Mid-Terms Aftermath

As you raise your capabilities and capacities to judge the duality of situations, this gives you a greater sense of sacred neutrality

That this Awareness is now prepared to present a message in regards to the events and circumstances that have been going on over the last several months, and particularly that which has now occurred because of the election, the mid-term elections, in the United States of America. Many may note, and have perhaps even questioned, why this Awareness was not available before-hand to make predictions, to state who was to be the leader or the winner of the elections. You have noted that by this Awareness not being present, that it left a gap if you will, a gap for each of you to step into. For this Awareness is not a source that will predict results and outcomes. Quite honestly there are so many timelines available, it would have been unfair to those of you who were involved in the elections, and watching the events that were unfolding, to have presented to you, by the nature of predictions, a timeline for you to choose.

This was your responsibility, not that of this Awareness. But it is the seeder of consciousness. It is that which would present to you, thoughts, ideas, information, energies, for you each to determine and decide for yourselves: how you were involved, where you were involved, what you were choosing to be involved with, which leader or group you wished to support. This Awareness can say to you, this is part of the responsibility of each of you, and indeed generally of humanity itself, to start discerning more and more between the bipolar choices that are available.

Your nation at this time is very polarized into two camps: those who you could call the Democrats and those who you could call the Republicans. Neither are right or wrong. It is as this Awareness has said so often, simply two different positions to come from. As you raise your capabilities and capacities to judge the duality of situations, rising above either choice and seeing both for what they are, this gives you a greater sense of sacred neutrality. Of balance. Of centeredness. And you do not have to then invest your energies for or against one side over the other. For you will see where both are coming from on the whole, positions of belief, in that there are the two camps that are presented, and many believe this camp, the lefties, or that camp, the righties, the Liberals or the Conservatives. But it is of course not as simple as that.

What this Awareness would say of the elections is it is part of a much bigger plan than anything that Fox News or ABC or CNN and or any of the controlled media, could present to you. Remember that the role of the controlled media, the propaganda press, is to harness a reaction towards that which they would wish to see happen, and in this case, this means largely a left-wing progressive liberal type of approach. But, as part of the bigger picture, you would have to see that there is more to it than simply a humanitarian stance on the part of left-wingers who feel they have the moral high ground, and who are the representatives of humanity, and those who hold humanitarian principles.

There is also that which is controlled from the shadow realms of this party and you have heard the term 'deep state' mentioned many times over the last several months, perhaps several years. And the ones who are the liberals are not any longer the ones who were the Liberal party of John F. Kennedy, for example. This is a new group altogether, and this Awareness will say that there is a hidden agenda behind these ones largely. But then you have Donald Trump and the new Republicans that are coming forward.

Of course, the controlled media, the propaganda press, has painted Donald Trump in very negative terms. And those who hold the humanitarian values, are led to believe that he is one who will destroy your country, who does not pay attention to humanitarian principles or causes. And that it is all something more personal, very ego driven on his part, that fuels him, that runs him. This would be inaccurate. For this man is one who has seen for a long time what is really going on, has known about the 'deep state' for some time.

Remember if you will that 'deep state' is a relatively new term for a phenomenon that has been out there for a long time. Previously these shadow ones, this shadow government, this shadow power, was known as the New World Order. Now they are called the globalists. Previously such terms as the cabal, the powers that be, the elites, the illuminati, and many other terms have been used for what is now being referred to as 'deep state'. But what this Awareness would say is that those who have been perceptive and available have long known that there is a hidden power behind politics.

The two-party system that you have, which is mainly Democrat versus Republican, is that which has been created over the years of marshaling the populace into channels that could be easily controlled. And, that previously, both parties were held by the same background group, the hidden hand of the 'deep state', the elites, the dark cabal.

Donald Trump even, was thought to be one of two choices, but that both were still controlled by this hidden hand. Until he pulled a fast one on them. For it is seen that while

Donald Trump did play the game for many years and many decades even, to present himself in a way that was acceptable by those who are the elites, when he was chosen finally as president this is when he deviated and shifted. And, to a degree showed his hand somewhat, as not one who is himself controlled by the hidden hand as it used to be, where both parties, and leaders of both parties, still had the same boss, worked for the same Masters. This took 'deep state' completely off guard, and there has been since then a reaction to this one. You know this reaction. This Awareness does not need to go down that road.

But, this Awareness will say that Donald Trump is not who he seems to be, in that he is not a servant for the hidden hand, he is not one who is simply playing the status quo. He is a champion of spirit for the shift in consciousness that is happening. His knowledge and his awareness of the bigger picture is great indeed although he very seldom shows much. And, it is so that in this time where the media and the press are still controlled, where it is fake news, and that these ones have an agenda against Trump and the new Republicans, it is also so that this is starting to break apart.

It may seem from the results of the elections, the mid-term elections that were held just the other day, that a situation has now been created that gives power to the Democratic Party, because they have won your house of Representatives. And yet this Awareness can say to you that this too was part, and is part of, the bigger plan. And many pieces are now in place for certain actions to take place that Donald Trump and his group, including that which is known as Q and Qanon, that they have been very diligently and behind the scenes putting pieces together, pieces in place, for this time. And now it is all go.

Many have heard the announcement today, but a few hours ago, that Donald Trump has fired Jeffrey Sessions. This is not actually what occurred. Indeed, Donald Trump did ask for his resignation, but it was not a firing based on that which has played itself out over the last months of an antagonism between these two men. But rather because Donald Trump is ready to go to the next level, and that Jeffrey Sessions played his role and played it admirably. He was behind many of the investigations that have led to the sealed indictments that are there waiting to be served. He, Jeffrey Sessions, is the one who is behind setting up certain factors in the justice system that will now be addressed, but he was never to be the one, the firebrand that would initiate. His role was to prepare things, and he has served that role and served it well.

There is actually great appreciation by Donald Trump for the efforts of Jeffrey Sessions, and you are not to be misled by those open and public confrontations between these two, for that was play acting. This will become more apparent in the future, and history will regard Jeffrey Sessions as one who was most involved in setting up circumstances that would lead to the actions that are coming. But, another is needed who will be the firebrand, who will take the torch up and light the fuse. This is still playing itself out.

But this Awareness presents this only as a way to help individuals understand how hidden many of the actions are, and how even though there may be a public display put on that shows antagonism and distrust between the two, this is only part of the game that is being played, has been played, and is still being played. This Awareness is here now, to inform you that it is all go. Actions will now take place over the several days, weeks, and months ahead. And this will cause a huge reaction in your government, and in your nation as well.

That many will not know how to deal with things, and many will actually come out against the president even more then has been so. The Democratic Party will not roll over. Indeed, they feel they have power now and they will be able to stop this man Trump, they will be able to impeach this man Trump, and they will regain their power. It is seen that they will never regain the power they once had, not as it once was, not as they once were. As this Awareness said this is no longer the party of John F Kennedy, of Democrats who truly had humanitarian concerns and principles. This is a sham they have been wearing. But that which may come in the future will be far more authentic to the real humanity of the Democrats, of the Republicans, of the people.

For it is so, the people of the United States are generous. The people of the United States do wish to help many who are not as well off. This is the true humanitarian nature of America and Americans. The fact that it has been hijacked and railroaded, and that those who present themselves as these liberals who hold these humanitarian principles, has been part of the deception and the long-term plan of 'deep state'. And it will one day again return to the truer principles, but right now what is being played out is this game of exposing those who have had hidden agendas, who work for hidden masters. And this is not yet at a point where it is obvious and seen by so many.

It is still at a place where the bipartisan nature of politics is not being met and it is indeed polarized instead. And it is one side against another. But this is similar to the condition of humanity at this time, where dualistic principles hold it must be this way or that way, instead of being able to assume the higher position; to observe, to understand that these are simply positions, this is all that which is unfolding. Furthermore, this Awareness, several years ago, did suggest that the period from 2017 to 2020 would be very critical. This is where the true battle would take place over this time frame and it is so.

Remember therefore that you are only slightly beyond halfway through that period of time. And then as you finish off the year 2018 with the monumental events that have occurred up until now, look forward, if you will then, to the year ahead 2019. There is still more to be achieved, the battle will still rage. And it is why this Awareness would still say do not simply judge Trump because of the dualistic presentation of this man by the controlled media and press, or the onslaught by the ultra-left-wing Democratic Party, but rather by his actions.

Several years ago, indeed a decade ago, this Awareness was asked the question about Barack Obama. And this at a time when he had won his campaign to be the leader of the Democratic Party against Hillary Clinton. It was a very antagonistic period. But many believed that this man Barack Obama, the first black man to be elected as president of the United States, would make a huge difference. He would lead the nation forward, he would be the Messiah, the Savior, the Avatar of the rise to the light. But it did not prove to be so. But at that time this Awareness said do not judge this man only by his words, but by his actions. And that history would one day do exactly this, that he would be judged by his actions. One can see through the history of his presidency that he was involved with certain actions and peoples that have shown him to be other than who he seemed to be before he was elected president. History will still decide this, in the sense of deciding whether he was one who served the light or the dark.

But this Awareness now says to you, do not judge Donald Trump only by his words either, but rather by his actions. He has come at a time of great difficulty and transition not only in America but globally as well, as well as the collective of humanity. He has come to serve a much greater purpose. And even though many judge him at this time negatively and would condemn him for his words, the actions of this man have already proven where his intent is. Therefore, as with Barack Obama, this Awareness says do not judge him simply by his words, but by his actions.

There is much that is unfolding now, and as already stated the next few days, the next few weeks, will be very intense. Remember that the energies of this month from an astrological point of view are the energies of the truth being given, the truth being brought forth and the truth shall set you free. Remember this in the next few days, weeks, and months as the turbulence rolls into 2019. These are the most critical of times, these are the best of times, and these are the worst of times. And it is so important during these times, for you to stay centered, to stay in the place of sacred neutrality, to attend the affairs of your own lives and to find that balance that you need to walk forward, during these most interesting of times.

The Freedom to Fly

Launch yourself into Divine Source and the energy of the Divine —

That which is Cosmic Awareness is available and greets one and all on this auspicious day of the 11/11/2018.

This Awareness would start by talking about this auspicious day. In that today's date is an energy that is significant because of the very event it originally was designed to remember every year. This of course being the conclusion of the first world war, that first global war that occurred 100 years ago. It is 100 years this year since the completion of that dramatic worldwide event known as the first world war, and it is of significance because 100 years is a significant time.

It is seen that those dark ones who love to use symbology, who love to use the circumstances of events, have targeted this date to engage in some heavy activities. It is seen that these activities could actually be very dramatic. And that their plan is to cause more than simply a remembrance of an event that cost millions of lives 100 years ago, to that which is being engaged in at this time. Actions at this time in history, are meant to shock the psyche of humanity and specifically in America, the psyche of Americans.

You already have events such as the wildfires happening in California. But at this time this Awareness wishes you all to understand, that you are in that which could be called the precarious situation. The energies that are being mounted at this time are energies of attack and assault upon the people of America, and indeed all people around the planet, is intense at this time. And it is seen that it will remain tense over the next seven days, the next week of your time.

11/11 certainly can be used to remember those who fell during that horrendous and evil war; a war that was manipulated and controlled by the dark ones to achieve certain goals at that time. Not the least of which was to offer up millions of lives, so these dark and vampiric ones could feast on the death, destruction, mayhem, and terror that was caused in that war. This too is part of their agenda if you will; to create mass energy that they can feed on. These ones remember, and specifically those who are not of corporeal form - this being the Archons in particular - need to feed off of the life force of the many that they use on the planet, the many who are enslaved to these masters at the various levels. Thus, when they have a war raging, this is a period of time for them where they can feast upon those energies that are being released in the death, chaos, and mayhem that is caused during a war. And the first world war was of a high nature for them.

That in their celebration 100 years later, part of the goal, by remembering those who have fallen in the defense of freedom as it is often put out, these ones are tapped into again. Remember they work outside of time and space and the irony, the irony of the remembrance ceremonies, is it opens a passage-way back to those events, back to the ones that died in the trenches, and on the fields. And these ones do take advantage, do feast again on those old energies. But they also have as their intent and purpose of creating a new round of suffering, chaos, and turmoil. And in this the energies of the past can help this to be sustained.

Of course, there is then a problem. Does one not remember the fallen? Certainly this Awareness would say the remembrance of those who fell is important. But what is equally important, is that it is not simply remembering them and honouring them, but also at the same time bringing it into the present, the present time, and then realizing and enforcing it will not happen now, and it will never happen again, for we have learned the lessons of that useless and terrible conflict. We see that we were controlled and manipulated. And we see that we have a choice in this matter. Therefore if any have a personal ceremony, or partake in the ceremonies of remembrance, please add to the remembrance of those who were used and killed off in that horrible war, and all other wars since then, this is their sacrifice for you to not ever experience war again. To energize that this is not simply about remembering those dead, that can be latched on to by these ones who use such principles as using time itself to open a passageway, they will not be available to this, it will not serve them. And even more it will never happen again.

As you hold this, believe the sacrifice of the many at that time will serve the many now in their awakening and in their intolerance of ever occurring again - this situational and manipulation control towards war - that it will never happen again, you will enforce and reinforce a new mentality against war itself. Therefore certainly remember those who have fallen in the service of their countries, but remember that their's should not be a meaningless sacrifice serving the hidden hand, but rather be the sacrifice of spirit in its drive toward shifting consciousness. Of creating a new consciousness at this time, that can acknowledge what once was but use the energy of that to create what will be and what is now.

This is the significance of this day in history, but it is also this day in the present. And as you hold that they will not be able to hijack this day, they will not be able to carry out their deadly plans, many of those plans that are planned already, they are trying to carry out, will fizzle, will not occur.

Can one prove this? How can one prove it if it did not happen? But one can say that you reinforced the positive. You held onto an energy that was not hijacked, that was not used against you. Therefore hold it this way. For this Awareness sees right now, at this very time, that you are all on the razor edge cliff. This Awareness has used this analogy before but it will now elaborate.

That you are on a cliff's edge that has two sides. And that the edge you are on, or that which is the solid ground you are on, is only a few inches across. And on one side the cliff falls away into the abyss. And on the other side the cliff seems to fall away but it is not at the same energetic of the abyss side of the cliff. There is something alluring to this other side of the cliff, the razor edge cliff. And yet it is a cliff. Both sides seem to present danger to you, as you stand there on those few inches of precious ground, not knowing what to do, you realize the ground itself that you are standing on, this thin wedge itself, is starting to crumble.

The question is what will you do? There are three options. You can jump into the abyss; you can stay on the crumbling ground below you and fall down as the ground itself crumbles away; or you can choose to launch yourself into divine source and the energy of the divine that is on the light side of the cliff. Remember, that you have a choice. Even inaction is a choice. And if you are paralyzed in inaction you will go down with that crumbling cliff. If you allow those dark ones, because they manipulate and control fear, and if you allow fear to dominate you so that you jump into the abyss, believing the lies and the deceits of those who are frightening you, that they will save you, then of course there is a set of experiences that you will have with this choice. But understand that the other choice, the leap of faith into the energies and the support of the divine, is yours as well.

And as you trust the higher energies of your own being, as you feel these energies out and know them, then the choice you make to jump into the energies of the divine are not really that of doubt and uncertainty, but rather of confidence, trust, and faith that you will be supported. And as you make this choice, as you take the leap of faith, you will feel the winds of the divine under your wings for suddenly you will have wings. And suddenly you will be able to fly. You will have the freedom to rise up above that level you had reached, to be part of the movement in consciousness itself that shows itself through your choice, through your ability to make that choice. That is the choice of the divine. That is the choice of spirit. That is the choice of the soul, your soul.

And as you soar with the energies, with the energies of love unconditional, the light unconditional, know you are part of the greater source itself. You are an expression of the divine, and the illusion you experienced on the cliff edges seem to be that, an illusion. Just as light is an illusion. It is quantified and qualified by the level of involvement in light, by the fact of the separation one experienced from source itself, from Spirit itself. But it is still an experience. Even the experience into the abyss, into the darkest energies, is experienced.

You are eternal in nature. Always remember this. And that even though the circumstances of life may be such that they are causing great fear, great tension, great confusion, and great chaos, still it is choice that keeps you here. Even though you may be presented with dualistic choice of the right decision versus the wrong decision, truly understand there is no right or wrong. There is simply the experience itself. If you are eternal in nature and the soul survives all, then even the journey into the abyss, even the journey into death will be survived. And even those journeys have their own lessons and opportunities to learn. Even though it is presented - these dark choices, these horrendous circumstance - as very unacceptable and undesirable, and yet still presented as if you have no choice, these are events outside of your control, that ultimately you do have control. Ultimately you can take action. You can launch yourself into the abyss or you can step out in confidence and faith into the open space of divine source.

This is the time you are in right now, to make this choice, to find yourself on the razor's edge cliff. And to know that you are not a victim, to know that you have a choice here, and that it is time to make the choice. To not simply be frozen in inaction and doubt. To truly step into the openness of the divine that supports you, that lifts you, that rises and raises you up, and it is so.

These are the most important of times, this time frame. This next week in particular, will present to you, to many of you, events and circumstances that can capture you in deepest fear and terror, that can make you think there is nothing that can save you, and that everything is hell-bound. Do not go there. Remember the words of this Awareness - you have choice. But the love and the divine energy of the source, of the divine source itself, are with you now. And even though events may occur in the next few days that are truly shocking in nature, remember that the divine is with you always. And you do not need to go into the illusion of horror and terror, you can see this too is part of the ending of things so that a new beginning can happen, a new birth take place.

That this is one of those apex moments, those razor-edged moments, where even though it seems that catastrophe is on both sides it is really not so. And as you choose the highest in yourself, for yourself, this is the action that will lift you up. And if you submit to the terror and the fear, that is the action that will bring you down into that level of experience. And even not deciding, even being inactive is still a choice of the nature of non-action.

These are challenging times, these are interesting times, but they hold also the promise of the divine. That which has been the corruption for so long is crumbling, is about to come down. And as you understand this and as you know your choice, is to choose that which supports you, that lifts you up. It will give you strength and confidence that which you know within yourself is your reality, and your choice of reality. And from this moment on all will change.

That this Awareness supports you in these critical and crucial times. This Awareness sends its light and its love unconditional to you all at this time and it is so.

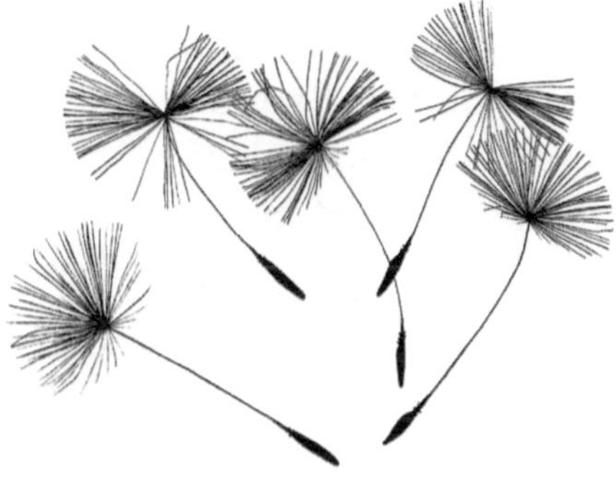

Honoring Choices

The new paradigm is Joy, Happiness, Pleasure, and Love

You are indeed in that most auspicious of places and spaces, and you are there by your choice. Remember this always, that your choices, which comes from your highest spiritual nature, that in the choice of being here at these most epic of times, you committed yourself before you entered into this time and into this space, to be part of the solution, part of the answer, to the dark ones, whose time has come.

That this has always been the intent, design and purpose of the Source, of the All and the Everything, which is the Divine Source. But it is part of your choice as well. As you see those events unfolding in the outside world, on that which this Awareness would call the perimeter of your circle of life, your circle of life, to please understand the ones that are there, the ones that are part of the events unfolding, are also there by their choice. And they are also sovereign beings just as you are sovereign. And even though it is tragedy and destruction and chaos they are playing in, it is their choice to be in this energetic chaotic field at this time.

This does not absolve you from reaching out and trying to help or to feel from them that they suffer, that you are empathic sensitive beings. But to please always understand that they, as sovereign beings, are experiencing what it is they have chosen to experience, their soul has chosen to experience. Just as you have as well! Therefore in the events that are unfolding in your personal life, look at those that support you, that lift you up, that give you joy and pleasure. It is time to realize now that the paradigm has shifted.

The old paradigm is that of pain and suffering and enslavement. The new paradigm is joy, happiness, pleasure and love. If you are involved in events and circumstances in your life that are giving you pain, that you feel you are suffering from, ask yourself, "Why am I choosing the old paradigm when I can lift myself into a new realm, to know it is joy, happiness, pleasure, love that really fuels me."

It may not come immediately. It may not be instantaneous. You may still find you are in pain on whatever level. But as you hold that this, too, is part of the illusion and deception, and as you hold that you have the right to choose otherwise ... and you choose the higher, you choose the pleasure, the joy, the happiness, the love. And it flows into your life along with much abundance. This too is part of that new paradigm: you live in abundance; you are creatures of abundance; all abundance flows to you continually and always. For you are in the higher energies now. You will begin to see this reflected in your life.

Many of you have wondered how to be a fifth-dimensional being, how to draw that energy in and do not have any idea of how to do it. And yet this Awareness has just explained it to you, has just told you how to do it; to step into that place of love, of joy, of happiness, of abundance. Hold it to be so. Hold it that this is how you are choosing to live your life and you honor those who choose to do it differently but it is not your way. And your truth is that you are a being of the highest order, the highest magnitude. You are being of sovereign nature. You are the Divine itself, the Divine Source itself, having this pinpoint focus personality experience. And if you are to have this type of experience, why not make it a good one? Why not hold that life is not the struggle, is not just about pain and suffering, is not simply about being a victim?

That you can choose every moment of every day what it is that you wish to experience. And if it does not quite work out that way, do not despair. Simply look deeper and say, "What is the lesson here? How is it that maybe my low self is not supporting me in this? Or perhaps I, the unawakened middle self, am still holding a belief that is inadequate?" That way, if things do not work out immediately, you at least have the means by which to figure them out, to figure out what you can do to change it.

Then remember also you are part of a collective, the human collective. And it, too, is going through this type of experience of moving from one paradigm, the old paradigm of pain and suffering, to the new paradigm of pleasure, of joy, abundance, love, happiness. But mistakes are still being made, or that it seems that there is a struggle in the choice, and many would hold that they're still victims, things are still happening to them.

And as they make such choices, you from your personal position can observe, can look at, can say, "That is all right. That is their choice. It is not mine. I choose a new reality, a different way. I choose to see Trump coming through, not simply as the man, as the lion heart, but because he is part of the shift in consciousness, part of the bigger plan, part of the Divine Source's plan." And you align yourself with this, for it is how you will move yourself into the personal experience of that which is the new paradigm, which holds love, abundance, joy, pleasure as the way of it. For it is so.

In the week ahead, the days ahead, despite what may happen, always hold that it is all in order to the Divine will, the Divine Source. You do not need to experience the depth of depravity or evil in the weeks, the days ahead if you hold that it is being shifted, it is being blocked, it is being diverted. And if, for whatever reason, you observe events that are of a dark nature, do not despair. Do not give in.

Remember, as this Awareness spoke earlier, remove yourself from the negative. Seek the positive. Hold it to be so. For you at least. And even if it is not so for others, this is not your responsibility, it is their's. You are only responsible for yourself, to create that perfect alignment with the Divine, with your spirit and soul, and to live it and to manifest it in your own life. And this will be an attraction to others. And this will cause others to come and say, "How are you doing it? I do not understand. You are doing something, you are living something here that I wish, but I do not understand." They are the ones that you can reach out to. They are the ones that are ready.

But in the meantime, focus in yourself. Know you are connected to the Divine Source. Know that there are the kindred brothers and sisters that are there and you are in contact with them in different ways. And they, too, are part of your truth and part of your reality as it is now and as it will be tomorrow. For you are the change that is the Divine and the Divine is the change that you are.

That this completes this session. In beauty it is. And it is in beauty that this Awareness sends to you, as always, its light and its love, its energies and its heart. And it is so. Be in the heart. Be in the beauty. Be in the now. And you will see who you are and what you are. And it is so.

Intensity

This is a time that this Awareness suggests that not only Sacred Neutrality is necessary, but Patience as well —

This Awareness states that at this time that it is a period of intense activity, intense energy, and intense change, that is happening. But, ironically while much of the change is there on the media coverage, the television, the radio, and even the press, much is still not seen, much is not known, as to what is truly happening. There is the obvious face of the information that is being provided over your mass media services, but much of this is controlled and manipulated, especially for those who have had control and power for some time.

There are many names for this group, the elites, the deep state, the cabal. Whatever you choose to call this group, these energies that are out there, that are behind the control and manipulation of events and circumstances, especially over the mass media, this Awareness says their control and their power is being broken down, is being challenged. Many are seeing events in their countries through those rose colored filters or lenses, that they will use when they view mass media, when they watch their 11 o'clock news in the evening. What this Awareness is saying here is be aware, much that is being reported is false in nature and is designed to continue the control and manipulation of the public, the collective.

This is important at this very critical time, for much that is being reported is designed to create tension and to create an energy of mistrust and even opposition to one who is elected legally as your president, the President of the United States of America. Many do not like this individual Donald J Trump. Many feel he is a despot in the making, that he is a wild and ridiculous man. But most of this is based on the perceptions gained by watching false media, by allowing the energetics to be manipulated and controlled by those with an ulterior motive.

As these are interesting times, as these are significant times, this Awareness asks one and all to realize that what is needed at this time is a neutrality. One is to observe events and circumstances but not necessarily take action yet. For at this time, much is being played out that is behind the scenes, and that which is being reported upon is not accurate or necessarily even the truth of the matter.

This Awareness would also ask all to understand in these interesting times, these deeply powerfully significant times, this is energy that is being presented for the purpose of great change. There is a shift going on at this time, a shift in consciousness. And this exceeds the bipolar effects of two parties standing in opposition of each other. For it is not as simple as the Democrats versus the Republicans or vice a versa. Even though it may seem the Republican Party is out of touch, it is seen it is through this Republican Party that there are more who are in alignment with the bigger picture and understand the actions of Donald J Trump and his crew, this including Q and Qanon ones, that this is part of the opposition to the elites, the cabal, the deep state.

Yet it is not obvious. And it is also so, that many think nothing of significance is happening and this particularly on the side of those who know of the corruption and the nature of those who are deep state controlled. This is a time that this Awareness suggests not only sacred neutrality is necessary but patience as well. That which is unfolding at this time is much more than a political struggle of two parties in opposition to each other. This is a turning point in the collective of humanity itself, and there are forces and energies that exceed the political arms of government or its opposition.

For those who are interested in the effects and results that this Awareness says, while it does not seem much is happening much is indeed happening behind the scenes, and to be patient now is important. But what will also be important, is when certain actions happen and these actions are seen as radical and overwhelming to many who were unaware of the actions that are needed, the actions that are underway. When these actions, when certain charges are brought forward, when there is a declassification of certain documents, this will mark an avalanche of information that will be released. The truth *will* be released, and many will find this too much.

Many will be challenged by that which is being released, that which is being exposed, and yet there are still right now many who are anxiously awaiting this. If one maintains a level of equality in this matter as an observer, coming from a place of sacred neutrality, those events that unfold will be the events that they see as moving things along. They will not be overwhelmed, but many *will* be overwhelmed. And the warning of this Awareness in these very turbulent times, these very important times, is that when such information is released and actions start to happen, do not be misled by those who oppose, those who speak the loudest, scream the loudest, that this is all corruption on the part of Donald Trump and his people.

Know within yourself that the truth will set you free and even though there may be turbulence ahead, more so than even now, this is necessary to bring down the corruption, to end the regimes that have been in power for so long. This is the turning point for humanity, and as such it is important to realize that which happens, that which occurs, is all part of the bigger plan.

You are part of the bigger plan. And this Awareness says to all be aware that which is unfolding is exactly that which the Divine has anticipated and planned all along. The timing of the Divine is not understandable sometimes but there is a timing, there is a release that will happen in its own way in accordance to this Divine Source and its timing. Know that the next month in the year 2018 and the year of 2019 will still be very turbulent. But it is important to understand that the turbulence and the upheaval that is occurring is all part of a bigger picture that is setting humanity back on its proper course.

This will always be seen in the future as the turning point, these very times you are living in right now. Understand this, and know this, and understand it is simply details that are now being worked out for the big change that is underway to manifest itself fully and completely. When things seem to be falling apart all around you, do not go into that deception, do not hold it that this is the ending of all. Simply understand this is the shift, this is the alteration of what has been, so the high energy of the Divine Source can once again enter into human consciousness and take away the power and control of certain dark force ones who have had this power and this control for far too long.

It is the natural order of things, and as you find your own balance in this release of the toxic energies that have so long controlled and manipulated, you will find yourself slipping into a place of your own adjustment, your own making. This is a place of great choice and choice in alignment with spirit can only be achieved through observation, through maintenance of a balance of a neutrality, a sacred neutrality, that will allow you to ride these waves that are crashing down, to survive the avalanche that will tumble down upon humanity.

There are many events that are underway, not all political. But the political events have their own significance and it is much more than simply two parties fighting each other. There are also global events that will take place and are even now taking place such as the incident recently in Russia between Russia and the Ukraine in the straits around the Crimean. These are all manipulations.

Stay aware, stay alert, have trust, have faith, know that the truth will come out, indeed it is coming out more and more each day.

This is the way forward for one and all to stay in this place of neutrality, balance, equilibrium, trust, and faith. And as you achieve this in your own life you will see it spreading out in front of you, both on a personal level, and as well regionally, as well as nationally, as well as globally.

These are the times many have been waiting for, and simply because things have not happened already, do not underestimate what has already occurred and taken place behind the scenes and even publicly. It is a great time to be alive and to know that the future is indeed a bright one even if one still must walk through the shadow of death before one reaches the valley of life.

Solstice Energies

Find a Peacefulness within you that allows you to celebrate that which is unfolding —

It is the 12th December, a few weeks before that which is the season of Christmas for one and all on the planet. Not all, of course, celebrate the Christian concept of Christmas. But all are nonetheless affected by the changes in the season, and that specifically which relates to the solstice in the Northern Hemisphere, the winter solstice, and in the Southern Hemisphere, the summer solstice. It involves the natural cycling of the planet around the sun. And that the seasons, even though some are not experienced as strongly as in other parts of the world, in other words around the equator there is not the differentiation that one experiences in the Northern Hemisphere or the Southern Hemisphere. Nonetheless, it is a very important moment and time of the yearly cycle of the planet.

The Northern Hemisphere, of course, is coming towards that period of time which is Christmas and many think Christmas is a religious event around the birth of the Savior, of the one later known as Jesus Christ, and it is the most holy of holy times for them. But it is all based on lies. It is based on the cycle of the planet which brings to the planet the solstices and equinoxes. And in the winter solstice, practiced in the Northern Hemisphere, that is celebrated in the Northern Hemisphere, there has been a confusion with the event called the birth of Christ, of Jesus Christ. Most of you understand and know this already. But this Awareness is saying that this year, this is a very important time, because of that which is about to come to a crashing end and that which is about to open up in the future, in the year of 2019.

Therefore, as you approach this Christmas season, understand it is perfectly alright to celebrate this season and this event, but to know that there are things on the horizon that are now looming into perspective, are looming into view. And this may be the last Christmas celebrated the way it has always traditionally been celebrated. This is not a prediction of a dire ending to things. It is simply that things are shifting very rapidly now. And you can see this on a daily basis when you view your television screens. When you see what is happening in Washington DC. When you go globally and you see Macron in France is under stress and the people are rising up, just as they are in London, and in England, and in Europe itself, it is all 'go'.

Therefore, the Christmas you are about to experience may well be a chance for you to reflect on the changing circumstances that are happening globally, that are happening within the psyche of humanity itself. And as you recognize this, and as you hold that place of sacred neutrality allowing that to come to conclusion which no longer serves, which is no longer the main stream of Spirit itself, that is also involved very much in the changes that are coming together now, you will see it will allow you to both enjoy the season of Christmas as you would personally celebrate it however that is, but also you are in alignment to the events and the shifts that are coming, and the cycles that are playing themselves out.

Therefore, even though this Awareness might say it might be the last Christmas that you would celebrate the way it once was, it is not saying at all that you cannot celebrate, that you cannot enjoy this time of year wherever you are, and understand that greater cycles are also playing out now. And it is not simply a yearly cycle that is coming to a conclusion as winter is often seen as an end time, a time of hibernation, but at the same time if you flipped it, it would be the time of awakening and energy in the Southern Hemisphere.

Therefore, if you understand these principles and you find a peacefulness within you that allows you to celebrate that which is unfolding, the cycles that are completing themselves, you will find yourself in a place of peace. And as this is the time of peace and a time of wishing to one another, peace and love and understanding. This is a time then for you personally, each of you personally, to simply be all right with yourself and with all that is happening, and all that is unfolding. For it is a time truly where humanity holds for a day or two, peace on earth, and goodwill to men and women, goodwill to one and all.

And this is again the true message of this season. And even if there is a shift coming and even if it is going to be quite different next year, and the year following, and then even more so the year after, it is still the time of peace on earth and goodwill to one and all.

Enjoy your Christmas however you choose to celebrate it.

You are a Magical Child of Spirit

Remember that the Magic actually is contained within you —

That which is Cosmic Awareness is available and greets one and all at this, the end of the year of 2018. It indeed has been a very important year, a very active year, and many of you who have been following the events that have been unfolding throughout the year, especially those events in the country of the United States of America, would say much has indeed occurred, and yet many would also say nothing has happened.

This Awareness would take you all now back six years, to an event that occurred in the year of 2012, which is the Ascension event that so many anticipated on December 21, 2012. Indeed an event of great magnitude occurred, but because it did not exhibit itself, strictly speaking in the physical, the transformation did not occur that many had hoped, where they had anticipated that they would become fifth dimensional beings on a newly-installed planet quite different from the old planet. Many were greatly disappointed and also at that time expressed that belief that nothing had happened.

Yet much did happen on that occasion whether you were in the North hemisphere or the South hemisphere, a crack opened and the door was pulled slightly ajar, the door to a more direct flow with Source and with Spirit. It was indeed a very important cosmic event, for enough had gathered on the planet to believe something would happen. That it did not quite happen as expected is part of what occurs often when one takes a leap of faith and then it seems nothing happens. But this would be erroneous, this is in error.

For in that opening of the door the energies of the Divine itself began to flow into the realm of the third dimensional realities of experience that exhibit for most the state of reality, their own, your own, personal state of reality. And although many did not see actual physical events that indicated a great shift had occurred, many did feel something; something had shifted or altered. But in the matter of faith and trust it is so that something happened, those who had just the slightest inkling needed to put this to bed if you will, so that it could come forward in greater strength with time.

At that time, this Awareness did express that something of great magnitude did happen. At that time, this Awareness spoke also of the importance of a nine-month period of gestation from December 21, 2012 till September 21, 2013. As you are all aware, that the human embryo takes nine months approximately to develop from the original seed and egg to the full-blown fetus, embryo, child waiting to be born, waiting to go through the last gateway to enter into the physical. And it is a time where much happens but it could be said much is unseen, for much that is happening is within the womb of the mother bearing the child.

And yet after that period of time is completed, after the nine months are completed, a child is born. Each child coming by choice. Each individual a focus personality of the soul that is expressing itself in this physical realm. Much is involved for this process to occur. For one's spiritual state is an expansive state indeed. To fit into a human body requires a type of process that allows the spirit to condense itself, to in a way make itself smaller and denser so it can actually enter into this human body that is about to be born. But all do it. It is part of that process of the seven gateways this Awareness has spoken of in the past. And how each gateway, if you will, represents a further condensing of the spiritual material into that which will fit into the human body.

Why is this of importance? It is of importance because it actually then explains how it is that which is infinite can be made finite, can enter then into this realm that is known as the physical reality of third dimension. Curiously, even though there is a condensing of the soul, the focus personality, at the same time this personality is still far greater than the body. And although it is housed in the body during that period of time which is the waking state, when one is physically awake, at night, or when there are times of rest or meditation, that soul can still expand outside of the body, beyond the body, and travel.

This is all part of the miracle of your being, that even though you might identify with the body and all things physical, you are certainly more than just the body. You are the soul expressing itself through this body and through this focus personality. And there are certain cycles that occur, that allow you to have experiences throughout the existence in that focus personality, throughout that life of the focus personality.

There are, for example the experiences of the child, a wondrous time, a time of innocence and magic. For most, this becomes controlled as the child enters school and enters the socialization process. In some you would say this begins immediately upon birth as one enters a smaller social unit known as the family. And that child is taught how to act in the culture of that family and of that nation.

But all children have a degree of innocence to them, 'trust and faith' in a manner of speaking, one can understand that the time of the childhood for each of you is that time where you have so recently arrived from the realm of Spirit into this physical body. And while you are here to have an experience in another level, you cannot be contained as that innocent, joyful, expression of the Divine Source itself. And that is why children are held in such esteem, and such importance, for they remind the adults who they are and where they come from.

Although this may be unconscious for most, still it is so, that children are honored, children are loved, children are held at the highest level by those who are the adults. And yet this is something often forgotten, and it is part of the state of affairs on this planet at this time that the sanctity and the magic that is the child, has been abused terribly.

It is not the purpose and point of this Awareness to speak on this too specifically at this time. It would rather focus on the fact that the child is magical, and that if the child is magical then by extension each human being is magical. And at this time of year, known as the Christmas time for you, this is a time of the honoring of the child, and the innocence of the child. If you would remember your own childhood, most, but unfortunately not all, will have strong magical memories of their childhood in a time when they still believed in magic. When they still believed a fat, jolly man could come down the chimney and leave amazing gifts behind. Is this not pure magic?

As you come into this period of time, remember there is a reason why this belief exists. It is there to help you remember that you are magical and you belong to a high spirit that is of the greatest importance, that is suppressed during the lifetime by most, that is not allowed to be the child in its innocence and trust, but rather must become the adult which is controlled and constrained by certain ones with authority and power. But this is shifting. This is changing.

That this Awareness now goes back to its discussion a moment ago of how this is the sixth year since the Ascension event of 2012. At that time, many humans had a similar sense of anticipation and uncontained joy towards an event that they believed would bring them a great change and great reward, that being what could be loosely called as the Ascension event. And many were somewhat disappointed that it did not happen to the full extent of their expectation. This would be equivalent to the child who wanted a special toy, but it was not under the tree on Christmas day. Still it is not saying that no gifts were delivered on that day, many were, especially the cosmic opening to the Divine Source itself. And sometimes what is needed is to be able to go beyond the disappointment of what did not happen, and rather to remain in that energy of the magic, and the trust, and the faith, that something very important and very magical did happen, as it did on that day.

And now you come to the sixth anniversary of that day. And this Awareness would say to you all, remember on the 21st and carrying it on to the season of Christmas itself, the 24th and 25th of December, remember the magic actually is contained within you, and that you hold it strongly just as the child holds it. And you are all honored by this Awareness and by Source itself as being the children of Spirit that have come into the realm of the physical at this very critical time, through your intent and through your choice to be part of the magical unfolding of consciousness that is underway.

As you look back to that event six years ago, you will realize it is your own decision as to how you held the energies at that time. And while many may have been disappointed and others may have been excited about what occurred, six years have passed since then. You can now look back in hindsight and can truly see how much has changed, how different it is on the planet now six years later. You will agree, no doubt, that so much has occurred in the last six years, even in this last year, this very exciting and entertaining year on the planet, and especially in the nation of America. And yet it is not complete, it is not done.

In some ways, this Awareness can say that by the way of cycles, this is the sixth cycling of the energies of that moment in time, but it is not the complete cycle. The complete cycle would be a nine-year cycle and this means there are still three years to go for that which started on the 12th, on the 21st rather, of December 2012 still has more ahead. And yet do not worry about this, hold that it will unfold as it is naturally meant to do.

What you can achieve is that you understand and know you are the flow of the Divine essence and Spirit that is unraveling itself on to the planet, that is exhibiting and presenting itself to humanity. And while events and circumstances play themselves out, and while it may be so the year ahead, the year of 2019 may be a very significant one, it is still part of a grander cycle, and that grander cycle is part indeed of an even grander cycle. And it is all the intent and purpose of the Divine Source itself expressing itself once again upon this planet, awakening the children of Spirit. Awakening you, each of you, to the highest calling of your own being, the trust, the innocence, of the child, the magic of Spirit. All of this is unfolding.

And as you pass through these times, as you walk from point A to point B in your lives, remember that you are moving forward, always you are moving forward. And that as you look at these events, stop being the cynical one who cannot see it in that positive light, in that air of trust and innocence. But rather shift to the child and the memories of your childhood, and the knowledge that children are here to show us the way, and that we, the adults then, are here to guide them and to protect them.

This Awareness includes itself in the 'we' are here to guide and protect. For that, too, is the function of this Awareness. To protect you, to guide you, to send to you the energies of the Divine Source, and of this Awareness. It is the greatest gift, it is the gift of the heart that always gives that this Awareness sends to one and all at this time of the season and year but at every moment throughout the year as well. And to remember this, and to call for this, is your divine right as beings of the greatest importance, as beings of spirit itself that have chosen to come here at this time, this very critical time, in the unfolding of the history of humanity.

To know that because you have chosen to be here, even though you may be going through many challenges of the physical, the aches, the pains, the fatigue, the depression, of having to be on this dense low grade energetic level that so many hold. It is still so that you have chosen to be here. And you have not been abandoned, you have not been left in the cold alone and afraid. The light of the Divine Source and the love of Spirit are with you always.

It is in your heart, it is in your being. And as you awaken more and more to the realization that this is so, it will allow you to step beyond that level that was once the accepted level of who you were, or who you thought you were, to a new being that is still in the birth process. Who is still developing as a being of the greatest height and depth and breadth of Spirit itself expressing through you, and expressing through your lives.

Therefore, at this wonderful time of the year when the light is returning back in the Northern Hemisphere that is the solstice event, or equally in the Southern Hemisphere when it is the opposite rather, the sun going through this cycle where it will shorten. Both north and south are uniting now and both solstices and both cycles are coming to completion to carry you forward into the birth of the New Year at this time.

And then as you do this, and as you step into the New Year, make your wishes. Hold your intent. Remember what this Awareness has said today, that you are the children of Spirit.

You are divine. You are blessed. And you are sacred.

Hold this within yourself, and even though the events of the year ahead maybe turbulent ones and great change may happen, if you hold on to the sacred knowledge of your own being you will ferry across these troubled waters and arrive at the distant shore. And it is there, it is ahead, and it is yours to attain.

Return of the Light

The Darkness is being brought into the Light —

This is the season of the Christmas the Christ mass, the Light of the Divine. This Awareness would say to you all, remember at that time and at that moment of the greatest darkness, that is when the light returns. This was a truth known and understood by the ancient ones, and many understood and celebrated the return of the light at the darkest time of the year.

Indeed, the ancient ones had edifices and temples and structures raised for this purpose. There is that structure known as New Grange in the Republic of Ireland, and in New Grange at that moment of the sun rising at the time of the winter solstice in the Northern Hemisphere in Ireland, the light of the sun went down a tunnel into the center of a huge mound and completely illuminated it. This represented the spark of the Divine Father impregnating the Divine Mother, Earth herself. And the life force from that moment of conception, spread throughout the land and beyond.

As you understand this cosmic universal truth, it would help you perhaps understand that even in the times of darkness, even in those times of pain and suffering, the Divine shines forth. And can enter into you and spark within you the growth of the Divine Child and the Divine Spirit within you. As you are that child, you will remember the trust and innocence of the child that you see in your own children, is sacred to the Divine itself. That is the promise of Source as it is always there for you.

A child intuitively remembers and knows this but it is forgotten as that child is conditioned and raised into the belief structures of a culture and a society. But as you remember the trust and innocence of your child, of you the child, and you hold it to be so in your life, it will support you and guide you, it will create magic in your life and miracles in your life. A child does not not believe in magic, for it is the naturalness of the child to believe in this fat jolly man who comes down a chimney to give gifts.

Indeed remember the disappointment that you may have had when it was finally revealed to you, as a child, that there was no such thing, this was an illusion, a lie, a deceit. Part of you died as the child who was moved into the more adult and mature expression of a human, to forget such childhood nonsense. But it is not nonsense. There is indeed a wondrous man who can come down chimneys and deliver gifts, for he is imagined and held in the psyche of humanity itself.

Magic is possible. Magic is the way. If you understand magic to be the expression of the Divine Source that is allowed to express itself in your lives and manifest in your lives. It is certainly tied into a whole belief structure of what is believed or not believed. What is brought to you in the beliefs of the culture and the society you live in, because it fits that society, that culture, that which has been manipulated by certain ones who have power and control or have had power and control for so long, too long.

And this is changing. And as you understand this is changing and the darkness is being breached, and the darkness is being brought into the light. And those who have served the darkness will have dilemma, for they will have to face the light. Or depart. That which is seen by this Awareness is exactly what is occurring now.

The light is coming. And the darkness is breached. And those who would try to serve the dark ones can no longer continue this in the light of day, in the light of Source, and in the light of Spirit. As you are part of Source and part of the Spirit, understand you are an anchor in this place, in this space, at this time. You are a conduit of this Divine Light, this unconditional love of Source. And that as an anchor, it is brought into you, through you, and into your environment.

You are that which holds in place the divine promise. Know this, and know it expresses itself first and foremost in you personally. Be open to receive, for this is the gift that does indeed keep on giving. And it is the gift you deserve. For you are the expression of the Divine Source having this experience, knowing it has chosen it on purpose and by design. You are part of the great unfolding of Source, at this time. And even though it does seem to be moving ahead so slowly, it is, in the view of this Awareness, an event that is accelerating day by day by day.

Hold it. Know it. Be it. And even though you may find the challenges there, and the aches and the pains of the body are there, let this sweep through you. Know that this too shall pass. It is part of the resistance that is being burnt away, that is being brought out to be released at this time. Know as you step through this, others will see that this is something of great importance, and they may not understand what is happening to you. But they will see that you are different. And they will come to you, so they can be guided to help them move through these troubled times, these interesting times. And know that this too is part of your purpose if you wish it to be so. And if you do not, then that is all right as well.

But what this Awareness would leave you with today is that you are in the darkness but the light is shining ahead. The dawn is approaching and it is of your choice, to step into the

light now and to know the truth of the essence of the Divine that radiates in you and through you. It is time now to remember this as the deepest truth of your being, and the truth that shall set you free.

This Awareness wishes one and all a very merry, happy, joyous, loving Christmas. To know that it is the celebration of the solstice that is happening. It is the promise of the Divine as it returns back at the darkest time of the Northern Hemisphere, back to bring the light. Know this is always the present and the gift of the Divine within you, for you, and to you.

Merry Christmas one and all.

A Wild Ride

There are two ways of responding—in absolute fear and terror, or with excitement and anticipation —

This is the beginning of the new year 2019 and this Awareness will say immediately that this will be a very eventful year, a very challenging year to many. But also a year that will provide new awareness, new insight, new understanding, into the reality that is life upon this planet.

Not only life in a general way, but life in terms of social culture, social means by which many live their lives, the beliefs, the patterns, the political parties they follow and trust. This is of course on a world-wide base that this Awareness is referring to here. But on a more national level, especially in America, this will be a year of great upheaval, of great shatterings, shatterings of those beliefs that have been held by many for so long, especially of course the political beliefs.

That this Awareness would say that this year will be like a roller-coaster ride. The last two years, 2017 and 2018, have been like the roller coaster ratcheting up the incline, advancing until it reaches the apex of the dive. And now you are diving down, plunging down into the depths. But it is a roller-coaster ride. The whole point of a ride such as a roller-coaster is to give great excitement and pleasure. But this is not how all would have it, and there are many who cannot handle the roller-coaster ride.

In terms of the events that this Awareness sees is happening this year, many of those events will shatter the beliefs and opinions held by some very rigidly. It must be this way, as it has been said, there has been two years of preparation, and now there is an acceleration as that diving motion takes place. Some would call this the quickening. But the point this Awareness would make here, is that this is a state of affairs that must now occur, because that which is hidden been hidden for so long is now in public sight.

This of course started in 2017 with the event that this Awareness has referred to as the Unzippering of America, when the solar eclipse passed over in America from west to east. At that time, an opening occurred that would allow that which was hidden to be exposed and to ooze out and become more and more obvious. This certainly has been taking place, especially over 2018. That is the equivalent of the motion of going up the incline of the roller-coaster until the apex is reached. And now, as said, the apex has been reached, the roller-coaster has gone over, the train has gone over the apex. In this plummet, in this quickening of times, there are two ways of responding; in absolute fear and terror, or with excitement and anticipation, because this is the part of the ride that is the most exciting.

It is also, as said, perhaps for many, the most frightening as well and the advice this Awareness gives for this year 2019 is to relax and enjoy the ride. It is imperative that as events happen around you that you do not get sucked into the vortex. Do not become overwhelmed by your emotions, by your thoughts, especially if you are prone to negative thoughts, negative understandings. It is important to realize that what is occurring is the death throes of the Deep State, and this is that which will bring many things forward into full light.

It is preparation even, for that which is coming, that which will start not in 2019 but in 2020. This would mean there is a year to go until 2020, but in this year of 2019 there most certainly will be much that is challenging, much that is overwhelming, much that is exciting and much that will challenge individuals. As the individual, having such a journey, this Awareness can only say, "Remember that you are the primary point of focus in your life." It is the perception of events going on around you that often influence and affect how one interprets the events and thus how one lives those events.

If you are suckered in and overwhelmed by events, especially those that are lies and deceit, you will find it most difficult to respond positively to the events that are happening around you. It is the exposure of the lies and deceit that is of primary importance in this year of 2019. For that which has been hidden for so long, but has been now exposed over the last two years, is of such a nature that the ground-set that many hold as their ground-set, their foundation of life and what life is about will be shattered, will be dislodged, will be obliterated for some. This would mean many will feel they have no grounding, no way of comprehending or understanding what is happening around them.

As this happens, the advice this Awareness would give is do not panic, do not go into that place of lost-ness, of being overwhelmed and lost in the events that are occurring. Step back, look to your own life, stabilize that life, stabilize your life. Hold and know these are the events that need to occur because of what is coming and those who have had power and control for so long are being replaced. They must be first brought down, they must be first exposed, they must be first shown to be who they are.

There are many who are involved, but this is a primary step to a new way of being, a new reality. In an earthquake, it is when you are stuck, that damage can be done. If you can be somewhat loose and mobile, you can ride out the shockwaves. It is when you are intransient in your beliefs and attitudes, and unwilling to change or look at things different that you will find you are the most challenged of all. If you understand this is the time of the quickening, this is the time of the acceleration of Spirit itself as it manifests upon this planet, you'll find that you can go along with the shockwaves and even enjoy the ride.

This year of 2019 certainly will be a challenge for many. But for those who are prepared and ready this Awareness does say the excitement you are feeling now, is of a nature that indicates you are attuned to the factors of Spirit that are playing out now. You are attuned to the inner understanding and awareness that this is that which you have been waiting for, for some time now.

Many have been waiting literally decades for the events to occur that are now taking place. And for those who are the newbies, those who are new to this, they too, you too, may feel this set of events, these circumstances unfolding, very profoundly, even if you do not have a historical background behind it.

It is not a matter of how long you have been involved. One could say that Donald Trump for example, has been waiting many decades for this moment, has known for such a long time the nature of the game and who has been playing it and who has been advantaged. And that he is champion at this time for this cause of liberation and freeing of humanity and of America, has had to be very patient indeed over those many decades. And now it is occurring, and he is part of that change and he is part of that train, that roller-coaster train that is on this wild ride. And he is taking many with him on this ride but he will not choose it for them.

Each must choose it for themselves, each of you must choose for your self how you will respond and react to the political and social and economic events that are ready to occur in this year 2019. And this will be global in nature. For many other nations will be deeply affected by the events that occur in America in this year, and it will launch many of those countries' response.

Indeed this is already seen. Those who are known as the Yellow Vesters for example, in France and other nations who are also adopting the yellow vests, are the groundswell, the ground movement and the people themselves are now awakening and the people themselves are now rising up. But with the events in America, spectacular and challenging, overwhelming and perplexing, the leadership does belong to America at this time.

That this year in particular will see the events that happen in America as the catalyst for change, not only in America but all other nations who are ready for such change. For humanity itself is ready for change and for each and every individual who is ready for the change. It has been a long time coming but it is now here.

Enjoy the ride.

Afterword by Cosmic Awareness

That which is Cosmic Awareness is available to speak a few words in conclusion to the book that is *The Unzippering of America*.

While this book contains individual opening messages that have been channeled over the last year and a half since that event in 2017, the eclipse of 2017, it is to be seen that these independent messages from this Awareness, although they can be read as independent messages, also constitute a greater picture. And it is when they are linked together and one reviews the material, it can then be seen that there has been indeed a bigger picture that has unraveled itself, presented itself one by one coming together in that which is indeed the bigger picture.

It is hoped that each individual upon reading the independent messages provided by this Awareness will both receive from those independent messages inspiration and understanding. But even more, that upon reviewing the many messages since 2017, since the event of the unzippering of America in 2017, that the bigger picture also is clear.

Further to this, it can be then seen for each individual, their own lives contain many independent events that have occurred, many strands that are playing out in an individual's life, and how it is possible to bring these strands together producing a tapestry that can be viewed from a distance or close-up. The closer one is to the tapestry, the harder it is to see the bigger picture. But when one steps back, one is able to review their lives in such a way that they can see the bigger picture. So it is with this book. So it is with life.

This Awareness would also take this opportunity to thank Callista for her efforts, her drive, her determination, and her inspiration in bringing the book together; to Richard Strauss for his creative imagination and his dedication to creating this book; and finally to Monica Brigid for her efforts as well in the process, in the proofreading, in the transcriptions, and in the support she has given.

There is one last individual to thank as well. This would be Will Berlinghof. For of course in allowing this Awareness to speak through him, for him being the Voice of this Awareness, it has presented the opportunity to present the information, the insight, the awareness, that this Awareness itself has been able to provide. This has truly been a project of the Heart and of Spirit.

Finally this Awareness would say that aside from the bigger picture that was presented throughout the book, there is indeed also the much bigger picture of Spirit itself. And the events over the last year and a half, while they have been amazing and formidable, are themselves but part of an even bigger picture that Awareness and Spirit are unraveling.

There is most certainly more to come...

INDEX

A

B

C

D

E

M

N

O

P

Q

R

The Purpose of Rainbow Phoenix Organization

We live in a unique and challenging time, with many seeking a higher standard of personal truth.

It is our intent and mission at Rainbow Phoenix to be a point in consciousness which will allow thoughts, ideas, feelings and emotions be exchanged amongst a collective of those who are seeking to step into their greater potential and the new reality that is now forming.

Rainbow Phoenix provides a vehicle for Cosmic Awareness to more efficiently express Itself on this planet. Cosmic Awareness is the Force of Consciousness that spoke through Edgar Cayce, and who speaks again today through Will Berlinghof as Planet Earth and Humanity go through these critical transformative times.

Rainbow Phoenix also offers a platform for the work of Will Berlinghof. Will brings over 40 years' experience to facilitate your personal growth and development process through the messages of Cosmic Awareness and also his own Counseling Method.

Message from Will Berlinghof

Since the December 2012 Solstice, the energies of Cosmic Awareness have expanded greatly.

Rainbow Phoenix seeks to accommodate these higher energies and messages and make them available to as many truth seekers as possible on this planet.

We are interested in reaching kindred souls who are here at this time to play their parts in the evolution of mother earth and humanity.

I provide frequent and time-sensitive **Messages**.

I offer **Readings** where you can have a personal interaction with Cosmic Awareness.

I can take you on a journey to discover **Past Lives**.

I provide **Personal Counseling** and **Spiritual Development Sessions**.

Take a look around our website and see if the information appeals to you. If you would like to join us on this journey, you will be most welcome.

www.rainbowphoenix.com.au

These are Magical Times.

These are Amazing Times.

These are Challenging Times.

But most of all these are Your Times.

Remember your selves
not as you are or have been,
but as you will be and already are.